THE ATLAS OF ANIMALS

Linda Sonntag

Consultant: Richard Walker BSc PhD PGCE

Aladdin / Watts
London • Sydney

©Aladdin Books Ltd 2000
New edition published in 2003

Produced by
Aladdin Books Ltd
28 Percy Street
London W1T 2BZ

ISBN 0 7496 5069 9

*First published in Great Britain
in 2000 by*
Aladdin/Watts Books
96 Leonard Street
London EC2A 4XD

Project Management
SGA design & illustration agency
Hadleigh
Suffolk IP7 5AP

Project Manager
Philippa Jackaman (SGA)

Designer
Phil Kay

Picture Research
Brian Hunter Smart

Illustrators
Stephen Angel, Peter Barrett,
David Burroughs, James Field,
Karen Johnson, Ian Moores,
Stan Peach, Jonathon Pointer,
John Rignall, Terry Riley,
Chris Shields, Rob Shone,
Stephen Sweet, Michael Taylor,
Myke Taylor, Andrew Tewson,
George Thompson, Dan Woods

Printed in UAE

A CIP catalogue entry for this book is
available from the British Library.

The author, Linda Sonntag, has written
for children on a wide range of topics
including the living world, human
biology and cultures and traditions
around the world.

The consultant, Richard Walker BSc
PhD PGCE, trained originally as a
zoologist, and taught both secondary
school and university students before
becoming a writer and consultant.

CONTENTS

Introduction 4
Classification 6
Animal Kingdom 8
Island Diversity 10
The Oceans 12

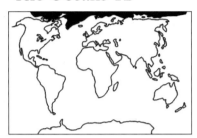

The Arctic 14

Europe 16
Forests and Mountains 18
Woodland and Farmland 20
Wetlands 22
The South 24

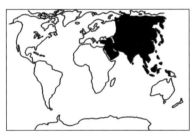

Asia 26
Taiga, Steppe and Desert 28
Himalayas and China 30
Tropical Forests 32
Indonesia 34

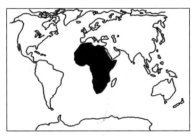

Africa 36
Savanna 38
Tropical Rainforest 40
Deserts 42
Wetlands and Mountains 44

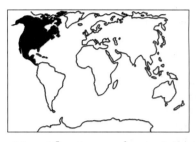

North America 46
Forests and Woodlands 48
Mountains 50
Prairie 52
Western Deserts 54
Florida Everglades 56

South America 58
Andes 60
The Amazon Rainforest 62
The Pampas 64

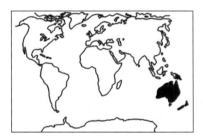

Australasia 66
The Tropical North 68
The Outback 70
The Great Barrier Reef 72
New Zealand & Tasmania 74

Antarctica 76
Glossary 78
Index 79

INTRODUCTION

Animals are found almost everywhere on the Earth's surface: across the continents of North and South America, Europe, Asia, Africa and Australia, on islands and in the oceans. But animals are not distributed evenly across the world. So why should some species (types) of animal live in one place but not others?

Who lives where?

Each species has its favoured habitat (place where it lives). Biologists divide the living world into major habitats called biomes. Each continent has some, or all, of these biomes, which include coniferous forests, tropical rainforests, deciduous forests, grasslands, deserts, wetlands, mountains and polar regions.

Biomes are shaped by climate – the average rainfall, the range of temperature and the amount of sunlight they receive through the year. Climate determines which types of plant will grow in a biome. Because animals feed on plants – or on plant-eaters – and because each species favours a particular climate, both climate and vegetation control which types of animal live in a particular area. Animals are adapted to survive in their particular habitat. For that reason, similar biomes share animals with the same characteristics. The desert jerboa, which lives in the Sahara desert in Africa, is as perfectly adapted to hot, dry conditions as the kangaroo rat, which lives in North America's western deserts.

Niche

Population

Community

Ecosystem

Biodiversity

Some biomes contain a much greater biodiversity – that is, many more species of animal – than others. Tropical rainforests, for example, have a much higher biodiversity than deserts. Being warm and wet all year round, forest conditions are ideal for plant growth, and the wide range of plants provides habitats and food for many animals. In the desert, only animals that can cope with heat, little water and limited vegetation can survive.

Lifestyles and living space

Wherever it lives, no animal exists on its own. Each animal species, or population, in a particular habitat interacts with others and with the surroundings. Different species survive in a particular habitat together because each has its own lifestyle, or niche, defined by its food, home and way of behaving. The community of different species, together with their surroundings, form an ecosystem. Ecosystems can range in size from a pond to a complete biome. Together, all the world's ecosystems make up the biosphere – the life found in the air, on land and in the oceans.

Biosphere

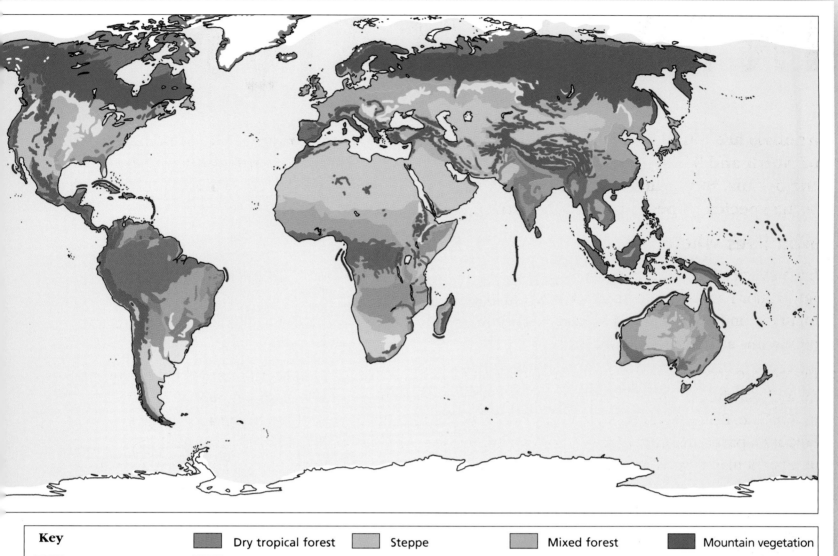

Key

Desert	Dry tropical forest	Steppe	Mixed forest	Mountain vegetation
Dry tropical scrub	Monsoon forest	Prairie	Coniferous forest	Reefs
Subtropical forest	Tropical rainforest	Mediterranean scrub	Taiga (coniferous)	Icecaps and shelves
	Savanna	Deciduous forest	Tundra	Sea

Who eats what?

The link between animals in an ecosystem is 'who eats what'. Animals eat in order to obtain energy to live. Sunlight energy is captured by plants, which are eaten by herbivores (plant-eaters). These in turn are eaten by carnivores (meat-eaters) that may be prey for larger carnivores. The route followed by energy as it flows from plant to animal to another animal is called a food chain. Because animals usually eat more than one type of food, food chains are linked together within an ecosystem into a complex food web.

Human intervention

The fine balance in a food web can easily be upset by human intervention. The rapid growth of human population has resulted in damage to many habitats and ecosystems all over the world by, for example, hunting, cutting down forests to clear land for agriculture and building, and pollution. Many animals are now threatened with extinction, which means they may disappear forever.

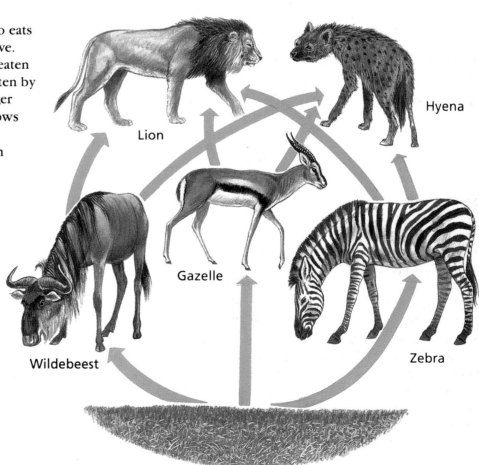

CLASSIFICATION

Sponges, jellyfish, dung beetles, lobsters, sea cucumbers, sharks, rattlesnakes, monkeys and the mighty blue whale all have something in common – they are all types of animal. Despite their enormous diversity (variety), all animals share common features that set them apart from other organisms (living things) such as plants and fungi. They use senses – such as sight, hearing and smell – to locate food, to find a mate so they can reproduce, to avoid enemies and generally to detect and respond to changes in their surroundings. They eat other living things, including other animals. Many have a skeleton that supports their body and enables them to move.

Numbers of animals

At the last count, over one million species, or types, of animal had been identified and described. Biologists believe that these represent only a fraction of the total number of species, and that there may be as many as 100 million different types of animal. Many of the species yet to be identified live in areas of high biodiversity such as tropical forests and coral reefs. Unfortunately, these are the areas most at risk from human activities, so many of the unknown species may become extinct before they are even discovered.

Naming and classifying animals

To make sense of the enormous variety of animals, biologists need an orderly method of naming and grouping them. The method they use is called classification, and it not only identifies and groups animals, it also shows how closely related animals are to each other.

Biologists classify animals by looking at their similarities and differences. Once this has been done, animals can be organised into groups of increasing size, from the smallest unit - the species - to the largest group - the kingdom - which contains all animals.

A species is a collection of similar animals - such as the lion - that are capable of breeding together in the wild. When an animal is identified as a species, it is given a two-part scientific name that comes from Latin or Greek. This system was created in the eighteenth century by Swedish botanist Carolus Linnaeus and is still used today.

o **Species**
Panthera leo, the lion, is like all other species - it is unique because of its individual features, and in the wild it breeds only with other lions and no other species.

o **Genus**
The lion and three other closely related big cat species are grouped together into the genus Panthera. All are hunters with slightly different lifestyles: the lion and leopard are found in Africa and Asia, the tiger in Asia and the jaguar in Central and South America. The lion is the only social big cat and lives in groups called prides.

o **Family**
Genus *Panthera* is one of several related genera (the plural of genus) that make up the cat family (Felidae). All 37 species of cat are lithe, active, mainly nocturnal (night) hunters that use their acute senses of sight and hearing to hunt prey. They live solely on meat or fish.

o **Order**
The cat family is one of eight families - the others are the dogs, bears, raccoons, weasels and otters, civets and genets, mongooses and hyenas - that form the order Carnivora. Members of this order are mostly meat-eaters that have sharp teeth and strong jaws. They either hunt prey or forage for carrion (dead animals). Some, like many bears, eat fruit as well as meat.

o **Class**
All the orders of mammal, including not only the Carnivora but also the rodents, primates (including humans), whales and about 20 others, belong to the class Mammalia. Mammals are unlike any other animals because they have hair and feed their young on milk. They are also endothermic (warm-blooded), a characteristic they share with birds.

o **Phylum**
Mammals, along with birds, reptiles, amphibians, bony fish and cartilaginous fish, belong to the phylum Chordata and are called chordates. Most chordates are known as vertebrates because they have a vertebral column (backbone).

o **Kingdom**
Finally, the many animal phyla (plural of phylum) - over 30 in all - make up the kingdom Animalia - the animals.

To find out how the classification system works, look at how the lion is classified as a member of the animal kingdom.

Lion
Panthera leo

Carolus Linnaeus
Swedish botanist Carolus Linnaeus (1707–1778) was fascinated by plants and animals. His life's work was to classify nearly 8,000 plant species and about 4,400 animal species, almost every plant and animal known to European scientists at the time.

Tiger
Panthera tigris

Lion
Panthera leo

Jaguar
Panthera onca

Leopard
Panthera pardus

Serval
Eptailurus serval

Cougar
Puma concolor

European wild cat
Felis silvestris

Spanish lynx
Lynx lynx

Lion
Panthera leo

Bobcat
Lynx rufus

Cheetah
Acinonyx jubatus

African wild dog
Lycaon pictus

Brown bear
Ursus arctos

Lion
Panthera leo

Meerkat
Suricata suricatta

Pine marten
Martes martes

Palm civet
Paradoxurus hermaphroditus

N. American raccoon
Procyon lotor

American beaver
Castor canadensis

Chimpanzee
Pan troglodytes

Common dolphin
Delphinus delphis

Lion
Panthera leo

Impala
Aepyceros melampus

Red kangaroo
Macropus rufus

Southern blossom bat
Syconycteris australis

Lion
Panthera leo

Harpy eagle
Harpia harpyja

Komodo dragon
Varans komodoensis

Edible frog
Rana esculenta

Clownfish
Amphiprion percula

Tiger shark
Galeocerdo cuvieri

Crown of thorns starfish
Acanthaster planci

Fiddler crab
Uca pugilator

Blue morpho butterfly
Morpho retenor

Octopus
Octopus vulgaris

Lion
Panthera leo

Portuguese man-of-war
Physalia physalis

Sponge
Clathria sp.

ANIMAL KINGDOM

The animal kingdom is the largest of the five kingdoms of living organisms – the animals, plants, fungi, protists and monerans. Perhaps the animals most familiar to people are the furry ones – mammals such as chimpanzees, rabbits or pandas. Yet, of the million or so animal species, only about 4,000 are mammals. In fact, only a fraction of the total – about 45,000 – are vertebrates (animals with backbones). The vast majority are invertebrates (animals without backbones). The largest group of invertebrates is the insects, a group that contains many species of beetle, not to mention all the other insect types. This classification of the animal kingdom is a 'family tree' of related major phyla.

Porifera (sponges)	Cnidaria (coelenterates)	Platyhelminthes (flatworms)	Nematoda (roundworms)	Annelida (segmented worms)	Mollusca (molluscs)
			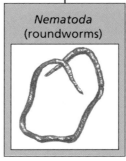	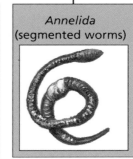	

INVERTEBRATES

'Invertebrate' is a general term to describe the 33 out of 34 phyla of animals that are not vertebrates. Invertebrates are very diverse and, apart from not having a backbone, share few common features. The major invertebrate phyla include:

o **Sponges** (phylum Porifera – 15,000 species)
Simple animals that live in the sea and freshwater, fixed in one place. They take in water through pores (openings), from which they filter out food.

o **Cnidarians** (phylum Cnidaria – 9,000 species)
Soft-bodied animals, also called coelenterates, which live mostly in the sea. There are two forms: polyps, which have a stalk at one end and a mouth at the other and medusae, which have a mouth surrounded by a dome-shaped umbrella. Corals are built by polyps, while simple jellyfish are medusae. Large jellyfish are colonies of both polyps and medusae. Cnidarians catch small animals using stinging cells.

o **Flatworms** (phylum Platyhelminthes – 20,000 species)
The simplest animal to have a distinct 'head' region at the front of the body. They have a flat body and include free-living forms found in soil, water and tropical forests, as well as parasites such as tapeworms.

o **Roundworms** (phylum Nematoda – 12,000 species)
Also called nematodes, they have cylindrical, tapering bodies. Found in huge numbers in soil and sand. Also important parasites of animals and plants.

o **Annelids** (phylum Annelida – 15,000 species)
Also called segmented worms, they have segmented, cylindrical bodies and well-developed body systems. Includes earthworms, marine ragworms and leeches.

o **Molluscs** (phylum Mollusca – over 100,000 species)
Soft-bodied animals, many with a hard protective shell. Most, like snails, are slow-moving, but larger, more intelligent species, like squid, can move rapidly.

o **Arthropods** (phylum Arthropoda – up to 30 million species)
Largest and most successful animal group, they have jointed limbs and a body covered by a hard external skeleton. Includes insects (six legs), crustaceans such as crabs, and arachnids (eight legs) such as spiders and scorpions.

o **Echinoderms** (phylum Echinodermata – 7,000 species)
Spiny-skinned, slow-moving animals with sucker-tipped tube feet, such as starfish and sea urchins.

Mammalia (mammals)

Placental mammals	Monotremes (egg-laying mammals)	Marsupials (pouched mammals)
		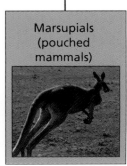

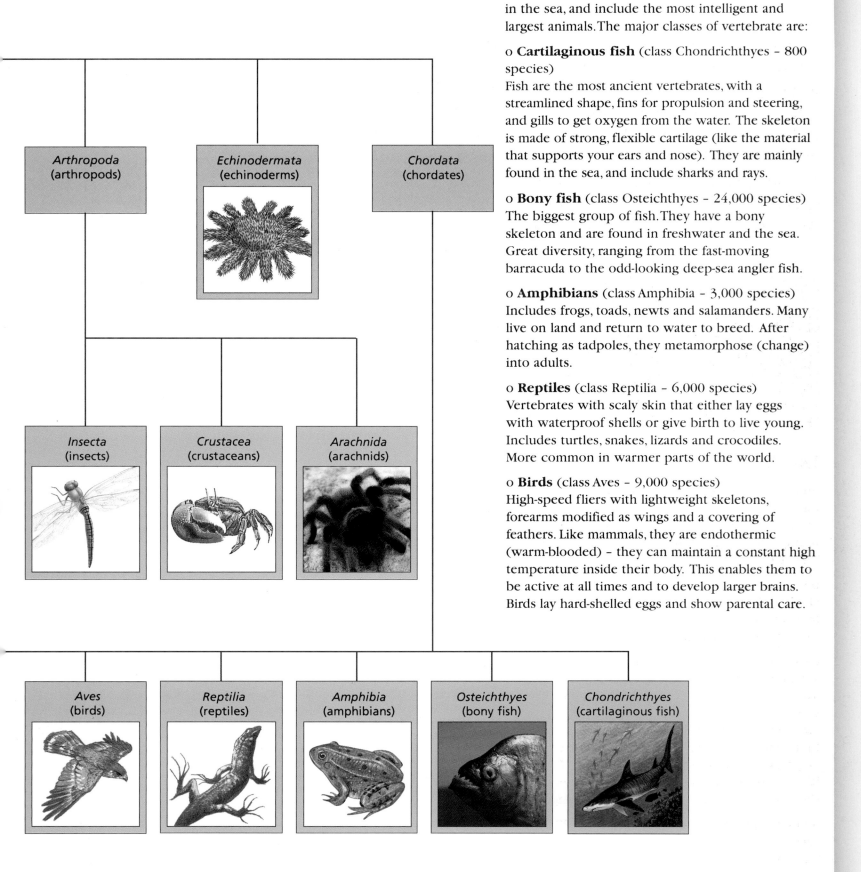

VERTEBRATES

Vertebrates belong to the phylum Chordata, and typically have a backbone, which forms part of an internal skeleton. They are found both on land and in the sea, and include the most intelligent and largest animals. The major classes of vertebrate are:

o **Cartilaginous fish** (class Chondrichthyes – 800 species)
Fish are the most ancient vertebrates, with a streamlined shape, fins for propulsion and steering, and gills to get oxygen from the water. The skeleton is made of strong, flexible cartilage (like the material that supports your ears and nose). They are mainly found in the sea, and include sharks and rays.

o **Bony fish** (class Osteichthyes – 24,000 species)
The biggest group of fish. They have a bony skeleton and are found in freshwater and the sea. Great diversity, ranging from the fast-moving barracuda to the odd-looking deep-sea angler fish.

o **Amphibians** (class Amphibia – 3,000 species)
Includes frogs, toads, newts and salamanders. Many live on land and return to water to breed. After hatching as tadpoles, they metamorphose (change) into adults.

o **Reptiles** (class Reptilia – 6,000 species)
Vertebrates with scaly skin that either lay eggs with waterproof shells or give birth to live young. Includes turtles, snakes, lizards and crocodiles. More common in warmer parts of the world.

o **Birds** (class Aves – 9,000 species)
High-speed fliers with lightweight skeletons, forearms modified as wings and a covering of feathers. Like mammals, they are endothermic (warm-blooded) – they can maintain a constant high temperature inside their body. This enables them to be active at all times and to develop larger brains. Birds lay hard-shelled eggs and show parental care.

Key

Phylum

Class

Sub-class

o **Mammals** (class Mammalia – 4,000 species)
Mammals are endothermic (warm-blooded), have a covering of fur and feed their young on milk. The majority – including whales, rodents, monkeys and bats – are placental mammals that give birth to well-developed young. Marsupials, including kangaroos and opossums, give birth to tiny, underdeveloped young that grow inside a pouch. The three species of monotreme – two types of echidna and the platypus – lay eggs.

ISLAND DIVERSITY

The islands of the world contain a treasure store of animal species. Many island animals are endemic – that is, they are found nowhere else in the world. This is because, over millions of years, they have adapted and changed to suit their unique surroundings. Unfortunately, people have now wiped out animals that are irreplaceable by destroying habitats and introducing alien species. The Galápagos Islands and Madagascar show us how unique island animals are.

The Galápagos are a group of volcanic islands in the Pacific Ocean, 1,000 km west of South America. All their wildlife arrived by flying, floating or swimming from the mainland. The dominant land dwellers are reptiles such as giant tortoises, lava lizards and land iguanas, and birds, including the Galápagos finches. All are endemic to the islands. The wildlife has already been damaged by introduced species such as dogs, cats, pigs and goats. Conservation is now a priority for the Galápagos, and tourism is strictly controlled.

Slowcoach

There are 11 subspecies of *Galápagos giant tortoise* – each adapted to conditions on its particular island. The shells of those on dry islands are arched high above the creature's head, so it can stretch up to feed on prickly pear cacti. On more fertile islands, the tortoise's shell is lower at the front as it browses on low-growing plants. Giant tortoises can survive long periods without food and water and may live for over 100 years.

Madagascar, the world's fourth largest island, lies in the Indian Ocean, 400 km off the southeastern coast of Africa. Its mammals are all endemic, including the monkey-like lemurs. Its 257 reptiles – 225 are endemic – include two-thirds of the world's chameleons. People arrived on the island some 2,500 years ago and began a process of habitat destruction, which has put much of Madagascar's remarkable wildlife at risk.

GALÁPAGOS

Wood worker

There are 13 species of Galápagos finch. They look very similar, but their beaks differ slightly according to their diet. The ground finch has a strong, sharp bill for cracking seeds. The insect-eating warbler finch has a more delicate bill. The *woodpecker finch* has a long bill. This bird is unusual in that it uses a tool – a twig or a cactus spine – to dig grubs and insects out from under the bark of a tree.

Sun bather

The *marine iguana* is the world's only sea lizard. It uses its powerful tail to propel itself through the water, and its legs to steer. Its sharp claws grip underwater rocks so that it can gnaw at the nutritious seaweed with its short, powerful jaws. Marine iguanas can be grey, green-brown or pink and may grow up to 1.5 m in length.

No escape

The Galápagos have the only *flightless cormorant* in the world. For centuries, the bird has had no predators to escape from, so its wings have lost the power of flight. It makes its nest of twigs and sea debris on the rocks and dives into the sea to catch fish. As its feathers are not waterproof, it holds out its wings to dry in the Sun.

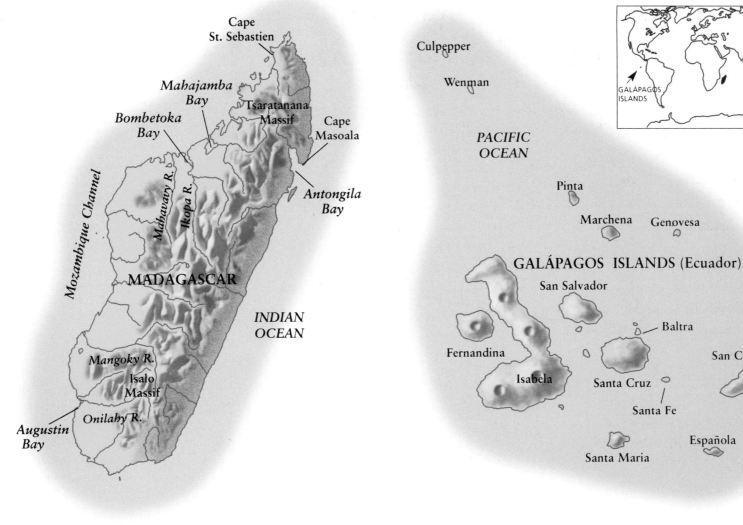

Cape
St. Sebastien

Mahajamba
Bay

Tsaratanana
Massif

Cape
Masoala

Bombetoka
Bay

Antongila
Bay

Mozambique Channel

Mahavavy R.

Ikopa R.

MADAGASCAR

INDIAN
OCEAN

Mangoky R.

Isalo
Massif

Onilahy R.

Augustin
Bay

| Kilometres | 800 |
| Miles | 500 |

Culpepper

Wenman

PACIFIC
OCEAN

GALÁPAGOS
ISLANDS

Pinta

Marchena   Genovesa

GALÁPAGOS ISLANDS (Ecuador)

San Salvador

Baltra

Fernandina

San Cristóbal

Isabela

Santa Cruz

Santa Fe

Española

Santa Maria

| 0 | Kilometres | 150 |
| 0 | Miles | 100 |

MADAGASCAR

Scent wand

Ring-tailed lemurs live in troops of up to 40
animals in the sparse forests of the dry south of
Madagascar. Females lead the troops, moving
through the trees to feed on leaves, fruit and
bark. Troops also spend much time on the
ground, walking on all fours with their
tails erect, patrolling their territory. To
mark its territory, the ring-tailed lemur
uses scent from the glands under its
tail. Rival males have 'stink battles'
waving their tail in the air like a wand.

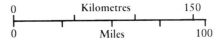

Hide and seek

The majority of the world's chameleons
live on Madagascar. *Parson's chameleon*
can change colour through blue, green, brown
and yellow. Its skin has several layers of colour
cells, which are affected by its background, the
level of light and even its mood, such as fear or
anger. Invisible to its insect prey, the chameleon
grips a branch with its pincer-like feet, then shoots
out its long tongue and catches its victim on the sticky tip.

Long fingers

The cat-sized *aye-aye* is a type
of lemur that leads a solitary
life in the trees. During the day
it sleeps in its nest, but at
night it emerges to go in
search of wood-boring insect
larvae. The aye-aye taps on the
bark of a tree, bites into it,
then winkles out grubs with
its long, slender middle finger.
Its large eyes help it see in the
dark and its sensitive, bat-like
ears detect the rustle of insect
prey. The aye-aye is now rare.

THE OCEANS

From space, the Earth looks blue. The reason? Over three-quarters of its surface is covered by water. The average depth of the oceans is some 3,700 m, and in places the sea bed plummets into trenches nearly 11,000 m deep.

As the Sun shines, its rays are absorbed or reflected by the surface layers of the ocean. At a depth of 200 m – the bottom of the sunlit zone – there is no longer enough light available for tiny phytoplankton to use. They need the Sun's energy to make food. These mini-plants are the base of the food-web. They are eaten by tiny zooplankton which, in turn, are eaten by small fish, which are eaten by sharks, seals and whales. From 200 m, the water become colder and colder and darker and darker until, at a depth of 1,000 m, it is pitch black. There is, however, a remarkably rich diversity of marine animals at all levels of the ocean.

The coastal waters close to land are rich in fish, and are the areas exploited by commercial fishermen. Where these waters meet the land, a narrow strip – the seashore – has its own variety of animals living on sandy and rocky beaches, as well as in rock pools. These animals are adapted to survive being covered and uncovered by the tide.

The oceans have long been regarded as both an endless source of food and a vast dumping ground for human waste. It is now clear that over-fishing, pollution by chemicals from agriculture and industry, radioactive waste and oil spills are having a severe effect on life in the oceans.

Jaws

The *great white shark* is feared as a killer in the oceans of the world. In fact, people are more deadly to the shark than it is to them, and the great white is now rare. Its torpedo shape and lightweight skeleton – made of gristly, flexible cartilage rather than bone – make the shark a fast swimmer. Its jaws have razor-sharp teeth about 6 cm long. The great white hunts seals, turtles and tuna, as well as other sharks.

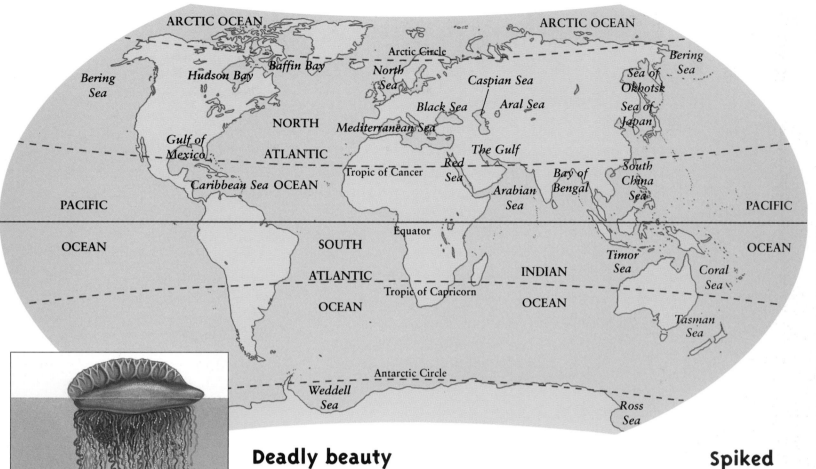

Deadly beauty

The *Portuguese man-of-war* is actually a colony of tiny sea creatures called polyps. Each has a different function. The polyps form long tentacles that hang beneath a gas-filled float on the surface. Some tentacles bear stinging cells. When a fish brushes against them, these cells release poisonous barbs, which quickly kill the fish. The tentacles then lift the fish up to the float, where the polyps digest it.

Spiked billfish

The *marlin*, with its streamlined body, sharply keeled fins and powerful tail, is one of the fastest fish in the world. It cruises long distances in search of prey such as squid, mackerel and tuna. In a shoal of fish, it strikes out with its spiked bill, then eats the dead and stunned fish. Because of its fearsome reputation, the marlin has become a common victim of 'sport' fishing.

Eight legs

The *octopus* lives in the rocks on the seabed. At dusk, it emerges to hunt shellfish. The octopus swims head-first by squirting a jet of water backwards through a funnel called a siphon. Well camouflaged, it ambushes its prey and stuns it with nerve poison. It can also squirt ink into the water to act as a smokescreen. It grips its victim with its eight sucker-covered tentacles, and drills through its shell with its saw-edged tongue.

Caring father

The *seahorse* swims upright and feeds on plankton in shallow, warm waters. Its independently moving eyes can spot prey without it moving, and it can change colour to suit its background. The female puts her eggs in a pouch on the male's abdomen, where he fertilises them and carries the young until they are born.

Musical crab

The male *fiddler crab* has a giant claw that he holds as if playing a violin. Fiddler crabs live on the world's warmer shores and dig burrows in the sand where they hide when the tide comes in. When the tide goes out, they feed by pushing sand and organic matter into their mouthparts. Females are quicker eaters as the males' claw, used for fighting and attracting a mate, is too big for feeding.

THE ARCTIC

The Arctic surrounds the North Pole and includes the far north of North America, Asia, Europe and much of Greenland. However, most of the Arctic is a massive sheet of ice floating on the Arctic Ocean. Conditions here are amongst the harshest on Earth.

In midwinter, it is dark 24 hours a day, the temperature drops to –50°C and freezing winds blast the barren landscape. Despite this, many animals live here. Polar bears and Arctic foxes are active all year, hunting on the large, moving ice floes. Arctic hares and lemmings burrow into the snow to escape the winter weather. Other mammals and birds migrate – they leave to find food in warmer parts of the world, then return to breed during the brief Arctic summer.

With 24-hour days, the ice sheet shrinks as temperatures rise. Snow melts to reveal the tundra – land where trees cannot grow and the lower soil is always frozen. The 50 days of summer are a time of rapid growth. Hardy, low-growing plants flower and attract nectar-feeding insects. Herbivores such as reindeer arrive, as do predators such as wolves. Both attract mosquitoes and other blood-sucking insects.

Long-haul flight

The *Arctic tern* has the longest journey of any migratory bird. It breeds in the Arctic in the brief polar summer, then flies south for summer in the Antarctic – a round trip of 32,000 km each year. This means that the bird lives in almost endless daylight. Arctic terns defend their nest and young by dive-bombing and hitting intruders, including humans.

Snow bear

The *polar bear* is a powerful swimmer that hunts on the ice floes. Stalking its prey on the ice, it is camouflaged by its coat, and the hairy soles of its feet stop it from slipping. It eats seals, reindeer, rodents, fish and dead whales. Polar bear cubs are born in dens dug in the snow. They are hairless, blind and no bigger than rats, but in just four months they are ready for the outside world.

Cold store

The fur of the *Arctic fox* is tawny in summer but turns white in winter to match its surroundings, so it can hunt and scavenge without being seen. Its thick coat, a layer of fat under the skin and its furry paws, help the Arctic fox survive the harsh winter, when temperatures plummet. To keep it going through the winter, the Arctic fox digs a cold store in summer, where it hoards dead animals and birds.

Sociable migrants

Snow geese are not always white – they can be blue or grey. They fly north each spring to breed in the short Arctic summer, where they have virtually no predators or competitors. The birds nest on the marshy tundra in colonies of thousands. Snow geese pair for life and raise the young together. The goslings grow quickly and within a month are ready for the journey south to the marshlands of the Gulf of Mexico.

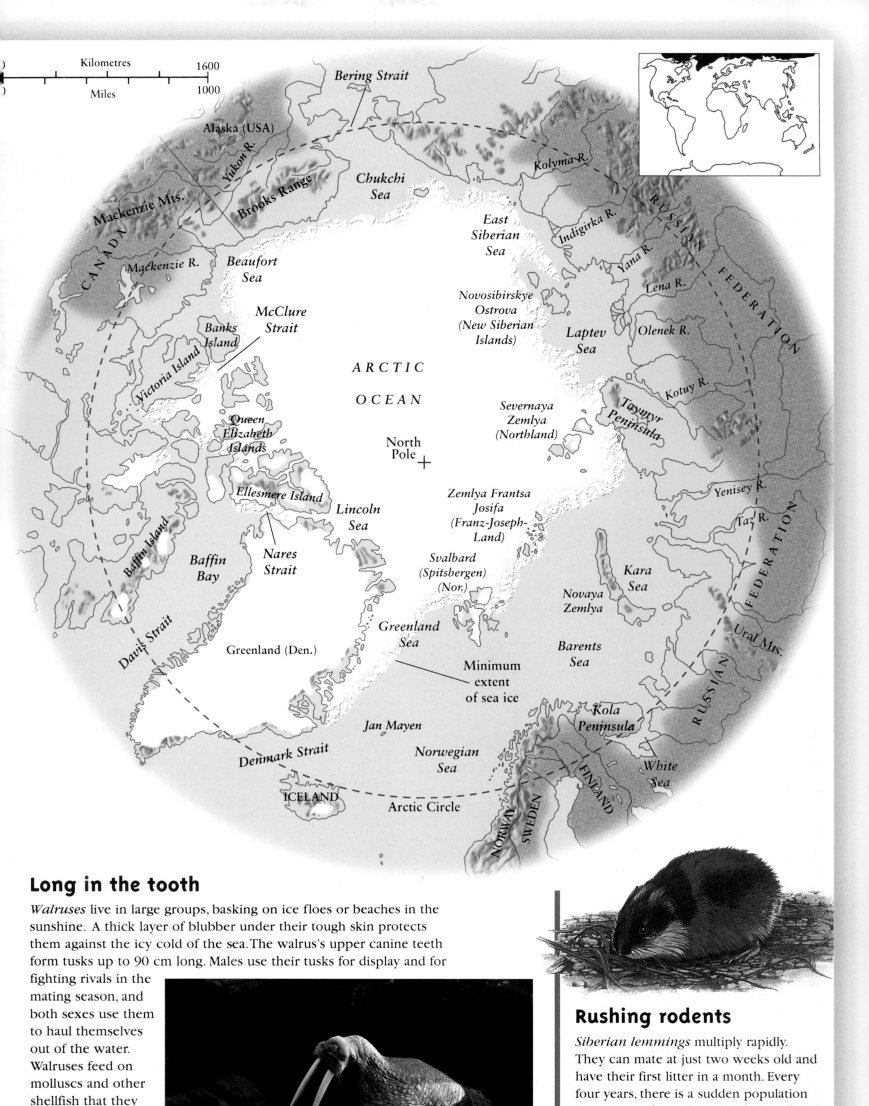

Kilometres 1600
Miles 1000

Bering Strait

Alaska (USA)

Yukon R.

Mackenzie Mts.

Brooks Range

Chukchi
Sea

Kolyma R.

East
Siberian
Sea

Indigirka R.

RUSSIAN FEDERATION

CANADA

Mackenzie R.

Beaufort
Sea

Yana R.

Lena R.

Olenek R.

McClure
Strait

Banks
Island

Novosibirskye
Ostrova
(New Siberian
Islands)

Laptev
Sea

Victoria Island

ARCTIC

OCEAN

Kotuy R.

Taymyr
Peninsula

Queen
Elizabeth
Islands

North
Pole +

Severnaya
Zemlya
(Northland)

Yenisey R.

Ellesmere Island

Lincoln
Sea

Zemlya Frantsa
Josifa
(Franz-Joseph-
Land)

Taz R.

Baffin Island

Nares
Strait

Svalbard
(Spitsbergen)
(Nor.)

Kara
Sea

Baffin
Bay

Novaya
Zemlya

Davis Strait

Greenland
Sea

Barents
Sea

Ural Mts.

RUSSIAN FEDERATION

Greenland (Den.)

Minimum
extent
of sea ice

Kola
Peninsula

White
Sea

Jan Mayen

Denmark Strait

Norwegian
Sea

FINLAND

ICELAND

Arctic Circle

NORWAY SWEDEN

Long in the tooth

Walruses live in large groups, basking on ice floes or beaches in the
sunshine. A thick layer of blubber under their tough skin protects
them against the icy cold of the sea. The walrus's upper canine teeth
form tusks up to 90 cm long. Males use their tusks for display and for
fighting rivals in the
mating season, and
both sexes use them
to haul themselves
out of the water.
Walruses feed on
molluscs and other
shellfish that they
dig from the sea bed
with their strong,
bristly snout.

Rushing rodents

Siberian lemmings multiply rapidly.
They can mate at just two weeks old and
have their first litter in a month. Every
four years, there is a sudden population
increase, so they migrate in their millions
in search of new food supplies. They leap
gorges, swim rivers and cross roads –
behaviour that has led to the myth that
lemmings commit suicide.

15

EUROPE

Lying between the Atlantic and Arctic Oceans and the Mediterranean Sea, and stretching as far as the Urals, Europe is the world's second smallest continent after Australia. Attracted by the mild climate and rich, fertile soils, Europe's dense human population has greatly reduced the number of animals.

Broad-leaved woodlands and forests once stretched across Europe in a band from the British Isles in the west to Russia in the east. In what is left of these, the wildlife is diverse and some large mammals, such as wolves and bears, remain. In the far north of Europe, where winters are long and cold, large areas of conifers are home to animals that can survive the harsh conditions, such as pine martens and wolves. Europe's mountains, the largest of which are the Alps and the Pyrenees, straddle Europe from west to east. They provide a natural barrier that protects the south from rain and cold winds. Southern Europe – around the Mediterranean Sea – basks in a warm, dry climate, where lizards and tortoises thrive. There are marshes and lakes throughout Europe, except where it is too cold or too dry, and rivers that wind down to the sea. Each wetland habitat has its own range of animals including frogs, fish and water birds.

Forests and mountains

Adult *European wild cats* live alone, marking out their territory with urine and scratch marks. They meet only in the breeding season, where several males may court one female, screeching and wailing all night. The female makes a nest in a rocky shelter or a hollow tree. When her kittens are three months old, they gradually learn to hunt rabbits, birds and insects. At about six months, the young are ready to fend for themselves. The wild cat was once found all over Europe but is now rare.

Wetlands

The *Eurasian otter* lives by riverbanks and the seashore and eats shellfish and fish. Its ears and nostrils close when it dives and its streamlined body allows it to move quickly through the water. Otters mark a territory with droppings called spraint. The young are born in a holt (burrow). The mother suckles them and drives the male away. She teaches them to swim at two months, but they may stay with her for a year. Numbers have been reduced by hunting, pesticides and road kills.

Woodland and farmland

The *Eurasian jay* lives secretively in its woodland habitat. This distinctive member of the crow family eats seeds and nuts, insects and small mammals, eggs and young birds. In the autumn, it buries a winter foodstore of acorns in the ground – usually one in each spot – and remembers where to find most of them months later.

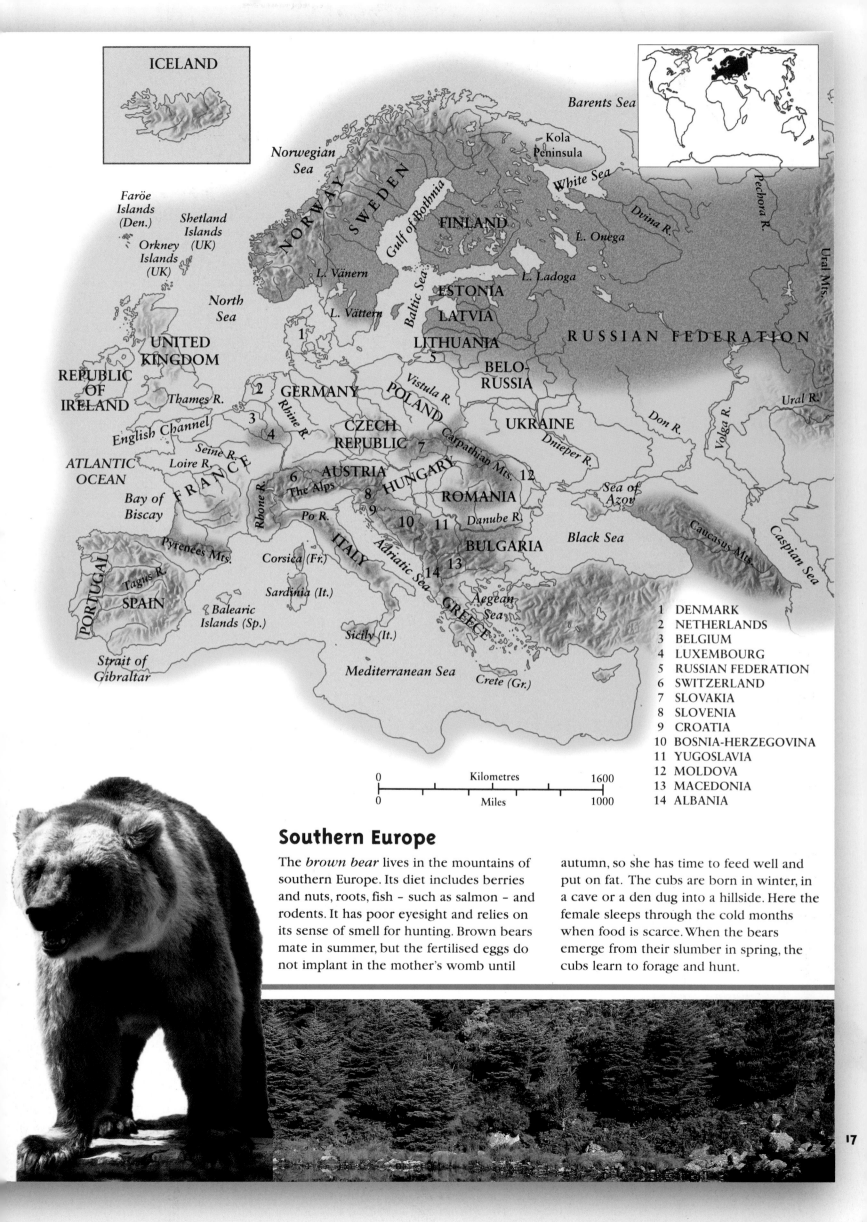

ICELAND

Barents Sea

Norwegian
Sea

Kola
Peninsula

White Sea

Dvina R.

Pechora R.

Ural Mts.

Faröe
Islands
(Den.)

Shetland
Islands
(UK)

Orkney
Islands
(UK)

North
Sea

NORWAY

SWEDEN

Gulf of Bothnia

FINLAND

L. Onega

L. Ladoga

L. Vänern

Baltic Sea

ESTONIA

LATVIA

LITHUANIA

RUSSIAN FEDERATION

Ural R.

UNITED
KINGDOM

L. Vättern

1

BELO-
RUSSIA

REPUBLIC
OF
IRELAND

Thames R.

2

GERMANY

5

Vistula R.

POLAND

UKRAINE

Don R.

Volga R.

English Channel

3

Rhine R.

CZECH
REPUBLIC

Carpathian Mts.

Dnieper R.

Caspian Sea

ATLANTIC
OCEAN

Seine R.

Loire R.

4

7

12

FRANCE

AUSTRIA

HUNGARY

Sea of
Azov

Bay of
Biscay

Rhone R.

6

The Alps

8

ROMANIA

Caucasus Mts.

Po R.

9

Danube R.

Pyrenees Mts.

10

11

Black Sea

ITALY

Corsica (Fr.)

Adriatic Sea

14

13

BULGARIA

PORTUGAL

Tagus R.

SPAIN

Sardinia (It.)

Balearic
Islands (Sp.)

Aegean
Sea

GREECE

1   DENMARK
2   NETHERLANDS
3   BELGIUM
4   LUXEMBOURG
5   RUSSIAN FEDERATION
6   SWITZERLAND
7   SLOVAKIA
8   SLOVENIA
9   CROATIA
10 BOSNIA-HERZEGOVINA
11 YUGOSLAVIA
12 MOLDOVA
13 MACEDONIA
14 ALBANIA

Strait of
Gibraltar

Sicily (It.)

Mediterranean Sea

Crete (Gr.)

0 ———————— Kilometres ———————— 1600

0 ———————— Miles ———————— 1000

Southern Europe

The *brown bear* lives in the mountains of
southern Europe. Its diet includes berries
and nuts, roots, fish – such as salmon – and
rodents. It has poor eyesight and relies on
its sense of smell for hunting. Brown bears
mate in summer, but the fertilised eggs do
not implant in the mother's womb until
autumn, so she has time to feed well and
put on fat. The cubs are born in winter, in
a cave or a den dug into a hillside. Here the
female sleeps through the cold months
when food is scarce. When the bears
emerge from their slumber in spring, the
cubs learn to forage and hunt.

17

FORESTS AND MOUNTAINS

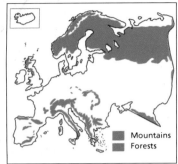

Mountains
Forests

Europe's coniferous forests, made up of spruce, fir and pine, can tolerate bitter winters and are spread across Scotland, Scandinavia and Russia. The seeds of conifer pine cones provide a rich source of food for crossbills and squirrels. In the summer, the forests are alive with insects such as midges and flies, which provide food for bats and insect-eating birds. Owls and golden eagles swoop down to eat birds, lizards and small mammals. In winter, the days become shorter and colder. Many animals hibernate or migrate to warmer locations. Only the toughest carry on the search for food during winter.

The Carpathians, Alps and Pyrenees, Europe's major mountains, sweep across the continent from east to west. With increasing altitude (height), the mountain climate changes and so does its vegetation and animals. It becomes colder and colder and also windier. The woodlands of the lower slopes give way to alpine meadows, above which are bare, snow-covered rocks. Only animals that can survive harsh conditions live here.

Sure-footed larger mammals, such as mouflon and chamois, move with ease over steep and rocky terrain. Smaller mammals and birds thrive in the alpine meadows in summer, when flowering plants and insects provide food, while birds of prey soar in the air.

FORESTS
Fighting pig

The *wild boar* is the ancestor of the domestic pig. It has thick fur and uses its strong snout for digging up food. It eats roots, bulbs and small animals. The males use their powerful head and tusks to fight each other when competing for females in the herd. A litter of up to 12 piglets is born in the spring. Unlike their parents, the piglets have striped fur to camouflage them within their surroundings.

Cone cracker

Crossbills of the northern forests raise their chicks early in the year when there is plenty of food. They live on spruce cone seeds, which ripen during the winter and open in spring. The crossbill hangs upside down on a large cone, then uses the two halves of its crossed beak to force apart the scales so it can lick out the seed with its tongue. The adults partly digest the seeds then regurgitate them (bring them back up) to feed their young.

Acid spray

Wood ants work together to build large nests of leaves, pine needles and forest floor debris. In winter, they hibernate in the soil under the mound to keep warm. They feed on other insects. If threatened or disturbed, wood ants fire a stinging spray of formic acid to ward off their enemies.

MOUNTAINS
Acrobatic flight

The sociable *Alpine chough* is a member of the crow family that bonds strongly with its mate. Choughs live in large flocks and roost in caves or under rocky crags. In summer, they live high in the mountains, where their strong wings enable them to glide on air currents. In winter, they descend to the valleys. They feed on insects, snails, berries and on the carcasses of small animals.

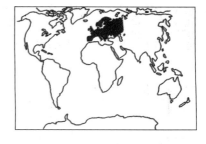

Sociable burrower

The *Alpine marmot* is a relative of the squirrel which hibernates for half a year deep in its hay-lined burrow. Many families live close together, in burrows about 3 m deep. In the summer, they feed on grass, seeds and fruits, building up vital fat reserves needed for their hibernation. Marmots begin to breed when they emerge from hibernation in the spring.

Mountaineer

Soon after birth, a *chamois* can spring across the rocks. It has strong legs and pads under its hooves to help it grip, and can make leaps of up to 6 m. Its speed and agility protect it from predatory wolves and bears. Chamois spend the summers grazing on high mountain meadows and the winters lower down in the woodlands, scratching around for shoots, mosses and lichens to eat.

Mole swimmer

The *Pyrenean desman* is related to the mole and lives near swiftly flowing streams. It has webbed feet and a long, flattened, rudder-like tail. It rests in its burrow in the riverbank by day and comes out at night to hunt for small fish, shellfish, insects and worms. It is at risk from fishermen and pollution of mountain streams.

Endangered hunter

The *golden eagle* soars on air currents looking for small mammals, birds, lizards and carrion. Swooping to the kill, the eagle crushes its prey with its talons, then rips it to bits with its sharp, hooked beak. Golden eagles nest on rocky ledges and usually lay two eggs. The first chick to hatch may kill its weaker sibling. In some areas, they are threatened by shooting, poisoning and loss of habitat.

WOODLAND AND FARMLAND

Woodland
Farmland

EUROPE

The European woodlands of broad-leaved trees are dominated by oak and beech trees, providing home, shelter and food for a rich variety of animal life that changes with the seasons. In autumn, the trees lose their leaves as they prepare for winter. In spring, there is a rebirth: buds, leaves and flowers appear, turning the woods green. Insects hatch out to feed on the young leaves and suck sap from stems. In turn, the insects provide food for birds, such as treecreepers.

Mammals also start to breed in spring, when food supplies are available. Deer feed on grasses and flowers that appear in forest clearings, squirrels scramble up and down tree trunks as they forage for seeds and fruits, while foxes hunt for small prey such as mice. Fallen leaves on the forest floor provide a rich leaf litter that is home to many insects, and also nourishes the soil. During the warm summer months, young animals grow and become independent. By autumn, as the leaves fall once again, the woods provide a feast of fruits, nuts and fungi. Woodland animals gorge themselves to prepare for the cold months ahead.

Although much of Europe's woodland has been cut down, greatly reducing habitat, woodland animals still manage to survive in hedges and copses. Foxes and badgers roam in fields by night and harvest mice nest between stalks of corn.

Not so fierce

Male *stag beetles* have huge antler-shaped jaws, which they wave to attract a mate. If a rival comes along, they fight. One may even lift the other off the ground, but neither is injured – the loser runs away. The eggs are laid in the soft wood of a dead tree. The grubs hatch and live off the rotting wood for three years, before turning into adults. Their life as a beetle lasts only a month.

Intensive farming

Modern intensive farming has severely reduced the variety of farmland life. Hedgerows have been ploughed up, removing the natural home of wild birds that feed on insect pests. Pesticides are sprayed to control the insects that feed on crops, but also kill many useful insects such as bees and ladybirds. To produce the highest crop yields, fertiliser is regularly added. Residues from the fertilisers run into rivers and lakes, causing water plants to grow out of control.

Sensitive nose

The *European hedgehog* is covered in around 5,000 sharp spines. If threatened, it erects its spines by tensing muscles under the skin. If danger persists, it arches its body, tucks in its head and rolls itself into a spiny ball. Hedgehogs hunt at night, sniffing out insects, worms, spiders and snails. They feed well in autumn, laying on fat to keep them going through hibernation.

Eurasian sparrowhawk

○ Flies swiftly on the lookout for prey.
○ Main prey – other birds, which it seizes in flight after a short, fast chase.
○ Takes its prey to a feeding post to pluck and eat it.
○ Lives in woodland and scrub.
○ Builds its nest in a tree.
○ Female is larger than the male, and is distinguished by the white spot on her nape.

European mole

○ Lives underground in a system of tunnels with a food store close to the nest chamber.
○ Short, strong arms that it uses like spades for digging.
○ Main food – earthworms that fall into its tunnels. It bites off their 'head' and keeps their body in its food store.
○ Poor senses of smell, hearing and sight, but has an excellent sense of touch.

Eurasian badger

○ Groups of up to 15 animals in one underground sett (burrow).
○ Often clears out the sett and brings in fresh bedding.
○ Poor eyesight, it relies on smell to find food at night – small mammals, insects, slugs, frogs, roots and plants.
○ A protected animal, but tragically, many are killed each year or meet with death on the roads.

Common blue butterfly

○ Males have blue wings. Females have brown wings with orange edges.
○ Caterpillar's food plants are vetch, clover, trefoil and other members of the pea family.
○ Adult butterflies sip the sweet nectar of wildflowers such as marjoram and thistle.
○ Groups of males drink from puddles, to get the minerals they need to build their hormones.

Stags and hinds

During the rut (mating season), *red deer* stags roar and lock antlers, competing with each other for females, called hinds. A successful stag can mate with around 40 hinds. After the rut, the stags leave to form bachelor groups. When the calves are born, their mothers hide them in a den, returning to suckle them until they can run with the herd.

WETLANDS

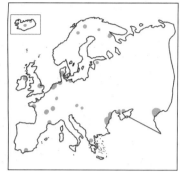

Europe's wetlands are found wherever land meets water. Pools, ponds, lakes, flooded areas next to rivers, swamps and bogs – all are home to an endless variety of creatures suited to life in or near water. Waterside plants, such as reeds and bulrushes, provide shelter for many of these animals. Wetlands provide important feeding and breeding grounds for many bird species, and act as vital stop-over points for water birds migrating across Europe.

In summer, wetlands are alive with insects. Many have two distinct stages in their life cycle, first in water and then in the air. Dragonfly nymphs and mosquito larvae are underwater hunters and scavengers. If they manage to evade predators, they emerge into the air. Other insects are taken by frogs and newts. Both these amphibians, and fish, are prey to birds such as herons, diving mammals like otters and water shrews, and large, sharp-toothed fish such as pike. In many parts of Europe, wetland wildlife is threatened because it is very sensitive to the pollution of water by fertilisers, the pesticides from farmers' fields and poisonous waste from factories.

Pollution like this is often catastrophic, destroying most or all life in the area. In addition, swamps and bogs are often regarded as wastelands that can be drained and built upon. Western Europe has now lost most of its natural wetlands; those that remain – such as the Camargue in southern France, and Coto Doñana in southwestern Spain – although protected, are still at risk.

Freshwater hunter

The *pike* is an excellent hunter. It waits motionless in weeds in ambush, then shoots out and grabs its prey. The pike's long jaws are full of sharp teeth – they even grow on the roof of its mouth. The upper teeth are angled backwards, so its prey has no chance of escape. Besides other fish, pike will take frogs, water voles, young ducks and moorhens.

Brilliant plumage

The *kingfisher* lives by clear, shallow waters that support lots of small fish. It searches for prey from a perch or while hovering above the water. The bird dives almost vertically into the water with its wings stretched back like an arrow, seizes the prey in its beak, then flies off to batter it against a branch before swallowing it whole. Kingfishers nest in burrows dug into the river bank.

Airy diver

The *water shrew* needs a constant supply of food to keep it warm, so it eats and sleeps in short bursts all day and night. It forages in the water for frogs and fish and on the riverbank for snails, insects and worms. As it dives, it traps a layer of air in its fur, giving it a silvery appearance. Its large feet are fringed with stiff hairs to help it paddle underwater, and it uses its tail as a rudder. Gripping with its claws, it can walk along the riverbed, nosing for food among the rocks and weeds.

All change

Noisy, water-living *edible frogs* eat insects, crustaceans and worms. In spring, males gather in ponds and croak to attract females which are full of eggs. A male jumps on a female's back and clutches her until she lays her eggs, then he fertilises them. The eggs hatch into tadpoles, which have gills like fish. The tadpoles develop arms and legs, lose their tail and their gills become lungs.

Born again

Male *dragonflies* establish a territory and when a female arrives, the male performs a courtship dance. The female lays her eggs on or in the water. The eggs hatch into larvae called nymphs that feed on insects, tadpoles and small fish. A nymph changes and grows for up to five years. When it is ready for the final change, it climbs up a reed, splits its skin and the adult dragonfly struggles out. The adult, which feeds in flight on insects such as midges and moths, lives only a month before breeding and dying.

Stealth and speed

The *heron* wades through water then waits motionless for a fish to swim by, or it slowly stalks its prey on the riverbank. Then suddenly it strikes, grabbing at its victim with its long, pointed beak. It eats fish, frogs, grass snakes, small mammals and birds, gulping them down alive. Herons nest in large colonies, each pair returning to the same nest year after year. The male defends the nest against rivals and shares incubating and rearing chicks with the female.

Wetland food chain

Wetland plants provide a food source for many invertebrates, including insects and crustaceans. The plants make their own food using the Sun's energy in a process called photosynthesis. Plant-eating invertebrates form a large part of the diet of the edible frog as it hunts in and by the water. The grass snake is active by day, sliding through the wetland vegetation in search of frogs and other prey, which it strikes and swallows whole.

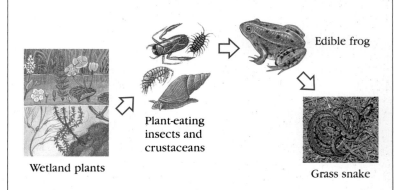

Wetland plants

Plant-eating insects and crustaceans

Edible frog

Grass snake

THE SOUTH

Around the northern coast of the Mediterranean Sea, the summers are hot and dry, while the winters are cooler and wetter. The main vegetation consists of scrub. Trees that can withstand dry conditions, such as pines, cedars and cypresses, provide food and shelter for many creatures, and nest sites for birds. Spring, when the climate is warm and the soil is still moist, is a season of abundance for flowers, flying insects that feed on them, and insect-eating birds.

Many birds will migrate northwards to cooler places before the hot summer begins. But some insect-eating birds remain, along with eagles and other birds of prey that swoop on reptiles and rodents, and the lammergeier vulture that soars on high in search of dead sheep or other carrion. Other birds, such as storks, migrate from Africa to nest.

Snakes, lizards and tortoises sunbathe in the morning to warm themselves, but shelter when the Sun gets too hot. Larger mammals, such as the wolf and lynx, are now rare because of the pressure of human populations.

The large numbers of people that visit and live in southern Europe have led to many habitats being destroyed. Land clearance for farming and devastating summer fires have caused further environmental damage. Protected national parks now include the wetlands of the Camargue in southern France and the dunes and forests of Coto Doñana in Spain.

Sticky feet

The adhesive pads on the *gecko*'s toes enable it to grip and climb up many surfaces, including glass. The pads are covered with millions of microscopic, hair-like structures that act as powerful suckers. Geckoes live among palm fronds, in crevices under tree bark, in rocky outcrops, inside cracks in walls and around houses. They rest during the day and become active at dusk, hunting by night for insects and spiders.

Saving the Spanish lynx

This medium-sized, stubby-tailed cat once roamed across all of Spain. The few *lynx* that remain compete with red foxes for rabbits and hares in the sand dunes and pine forests of the Coto Doñana National Park in southwestern Spain. The Park itself, which has extensive wetlands that attract storks and flamingoes, is also at risk because its vital ground water is being extracted for agriculture and tourism.

Cave seals

Mediterranean monk seals live in colonies in sea caves in the Mediterranean Sea and the Atlantic Ocean. They are the only seals that live in warm waters. There are now fewer than 500 of them left in the wild. Their numbers have been greatly reduced by fishing and water pollution, and holidaymakers often disturb the seals when they come ashore on to the beaches to breed. The seal's streamlined body and paddle-like flippers make it a fast and agile swimmer. Its main food is fish and squid.

Pine processionary moth

○ Spins a flask-shaped nest that hangs from a tree's twigs.
○ At night, a procession of about 100 caterpillars moves nose to tail along branches to find new feeding areas where they can feast on pine needles.
○ Seems vulnerable to predators, but hairs on the caterpillar taste bad so they are left alone.
○ Considered as pests in the pine forests of southern Europe.

Greater flamingo

○ Feeds with its head down in the water, filtering food with the fine plates inside its bill.
○ Eats protozoa, algae, insects, crustaceans, molluscs and worms.
○ Pink colour comes from carotenoids (natural chemicals found in algae and shrimp).
○ Nests in colonies of thousands, each pair building a mud nest and sharing incubation and rearing of their single chick.

Hermann's tortoise

○ Likes scrub-covered hillsides and woodlands near the coast.
○ Eats plants and insects.
○ Male courts by biting the female's legs and crashing into her with his shell while squealing like a puppy.
○ Female lays about 12 eggs in a nest scraped in dusty soil.
○ Eggs hatch in about three months.
○ Baby tortoises are independent from birth.

Fire salamander

○ Hatches from an egg in shallow water as a tadpole. Takes three months to develop fully into an adult.
○ If threatened, secretes (releases) a sticky white poison from glands on its back and behind its head.
○ May have yellow or red markings which warn predators that the salamander is poisonous.
○ Hunts at night for worms, slugs, snails and insects.

White beauty

Camargue horses live in the wetlands of southern France. They run free, but have owners who ensure their survival and tame some horses, using them to round up wild black bulls. The dominant stallions drive out the young males. Fights between stallions are fierce. Foals are born a year after mating and may suckle for up to two years.

Good luck bird

Storks pair for life and build a large nest in a tree or on a chimney pot. They return to the same site each year and mate on the nest. Parents take turns to feed the chicks with regurgitated frogs, insects, lizards, fish and worms. After about three months, the young learn to fly. At the end of the summer, the storks migrate to southern Africa.

ASIA

Asia is the largest continent in the world, covering some 44.4 million square km. It extends south from the freezing Arctic to the equator, and is separated from Europe in the west by the Ural and Caucasus mountains, and from North America in the east by the Bering Strait.

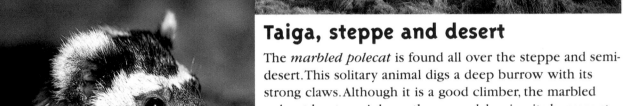

While much of Asia consists of rolling plains, a central highland region stretches from west to east. Called the Himalayas, the highest point is at 8,848 m. In the far north of Siberia, coniferous forests called the taiga have long, bitterly cold winters and are home only to animals that can survive the harsh conditions, like wolves and pine martens. Moving south, the taiga gives way to steppe (open grassland), where many ground-living animals are found. Most of central and southwestern Asia is dry desert, where camels and gerbils have adapted to the hot, dry conditions. The Himalayan mountains separate these barren wastelands from the hot Indian subcontinent and the dense tropical forests of Southeast Asia.

The rapid increase in human population presents a serious threat to many Asian species. The tiger, once widespread throughout Asia, has been reduced to small, isolated populations and may become extinct in the wild. In China, the giant panda, a symbol of animal conservation world-wide, is also facing extinction. Many other smaller and lesser-known species are also endangered.

Taiga, steppe and desert

The *marbled polecat* is found all over the steppe and semi-desert. This solitary animal digs a deep burrow with its strong claws. Although it is a good climber, the marbled polecat hunts mainly on the ground, leaving its burrow at dusk to hunt rodents, rabbits, frogs, lizards, snakes and birds. If threatened, it throws back its head, bares its teeth and curls its tail over its back to reveal warning markings. Then it squirts an unpleasant scent from glands under its tail. It also uses this scent for marking its territory.

Mountains

Musk deer are shy, solitary animals that live in the forested mountains of central and eastern Asia. No more than 60 cm high, they bound sure-footedly across rocks. The male has 7 cm-long canine teeth, which it uses to fight other males for a mate. The males also secrete (release) musk from a gland under their belly, which they use to mark their territory. Once hunted for their musk, which is used to make perfume, the deer are now farmed and the musk is taken without killing them.

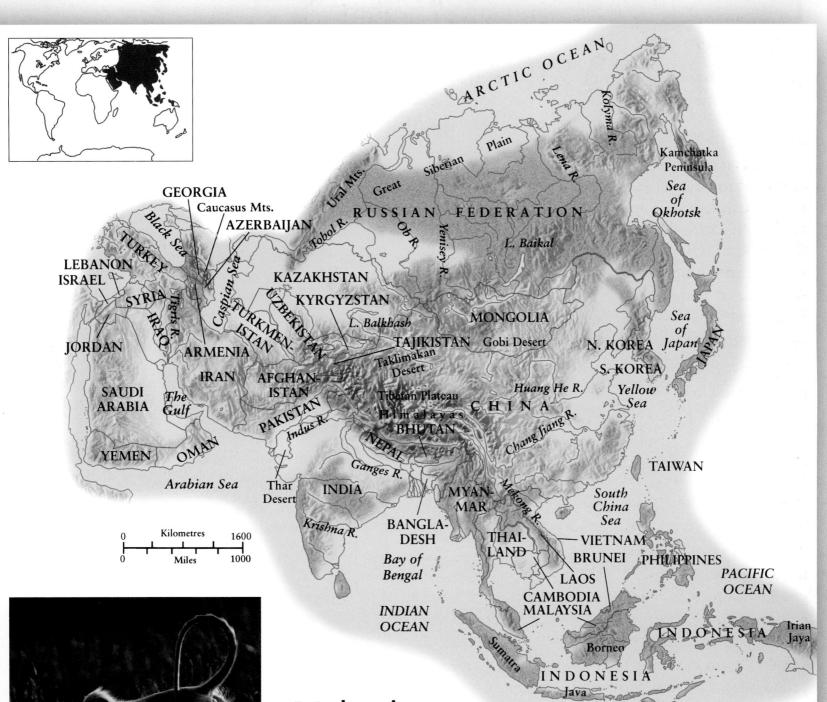

ARCTIC OCEAN

Kolyma R.

Kamchatka Peninsula

Sea of Okhotsk

Plain

Siberian

Lena R.

RUSSIAN FEDERATION

Ural Mts.

Great

Tobol R.

Ob R.

Yenisey R.

L. Baikal

GEORGIA
Caucasus Mts.
AZERBAIJAN

Black Sea

TURKEY

LEBANON
ISRAEL

SYRIA

IRAQ

Tigris R.

Caspian Sea

KAZAKHSTAN

KYRGYZSTAN

L. Balkhash

MONGOLIA

Sea of Japan

N. KOREA

S. KOREA

JAPAN

JORDAN

ARMENIA

TURKMEN-ISTAN

UZBEKISTAN

TAJIKISTAN

Gobi Desert

Taklimakan Desert

IRAN

AFGHAN-ISTAN

Tibetan Plateau

Huang He R.

Yellow Sea

SAUDI ARABIA

The Gulf

PAKISTAN

Indus R.

Himalayas

BHUTAN

CHINA

Chang Jiang R.

YEMEN

OMAN

NEPAL

Ganges R.

Thar Desert

INDIA

MYAN-MAR

Mekong R.

TAIWAN

South China Sea

Arabian Sea

BANGLA-DESH

THAI-LAND

VIETNAM

BRUNEI

PHILIPPINES

PACIFIC OCEAN

Krishna R.

Bay of Bengal

LAOS

CAMBODIA

MALAYSIA

INDONESIA

Irian Jaya

INDIAN OCEAN

Sumatra

Borneo

INDONESIA

Java

| 0 | Kilometres | 1600 |
| 0 | Miles | 1000 |

Indonesia

Some of Indonesia's forest animals have developed a way of gliding from tree to tree to feast on fruits, leaves and insects that are plentiful all year round. They include the *colugo*, a mammal also known as the 'flying lemur'. Although it cannot fly like a bird or bat, a membrane called a patagium stretches between its arms, legs and tail. This gets in the way when the colugo scrambles up a tree trunk, but spread out, it allows the 'flying lemur' to glide up to 135 m. The young get their first 'flying' lessons by clinging to their mother's stomach.

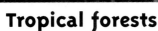

Tropical forests

Hanuman langurs live in groups of up to 20 in the tropical forests of southern Asia. The young are cared for by 'aunts', who relieve nursing mothers. A male may try to kill the young when he takes over the group so that the females will breed with him. The females gang together to fight him off, and sometimes they succeed. Moving through the trees or on the ground, langurs eat leaves, flowers and fruit, sometimes raiding villages for food. People put up with them as they are regarded as sacred; they are named after Hanuman, the Hindu monkey-god.

27

TAIGA, STEPPE AND DESERT

ASIA

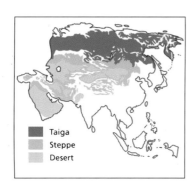

Taiga
Steppe
Desert

The coniferous forest that forms the taiga of northern Asia is the largest forest in the world. The winters are long and harsh, but the short, warm summers see an explosion of life. The trees provide a rich source of food. In late spring, many birds arrive in the forests to feed on the larch, spruce and fir tree seeds as well as the many insects. Birds of prey, like the goshawk, hunt these smaller birds. In autumn, most birds leave for warmer areas, while many mammals hibernate.

South of the taiga lie the vast steppes of central Asia. Here, the winters are cold and the summers are hot and dry. Spring is the most productive time, when animals start to have young. Smaller ground-dwelling mammals, such as susliks and hamsters, go underground to seek shelter from the cold and from predators, particularly birds of prey. The huge herds of grazing mammals that once roamed the steppe, such as the saiga antelope and European bison, have largely disappeared.

The central Asian deserts lie south of the steppes. Summer days are hot, but temperatures plummet at night, and the winters are often icy cold. Here, animals have to withstand not only drought but also extreme cold. The Bactrian camel, for example, has a long, protective winter coat, and is able to travel for long periods without water.

Hungry pack
The *grey wolf* can go for weeks without food, then eat up to 10 kg of meat in one go. It eats hares, lemmings, musk oxen and caribou, but as the grazing is poor in the Siberian winter, the larger animals are scarce and wolves must cover up to 2,000 sq km to find enough to eat. Hunting in a pack, grey wolves concentrate on isolating one animal from the group and dragging it down. A kill can feed the pack for several days.

Suslik

○ Sociable ground squirrel that lives in colonies of many thousands, with burrows sited close together.
○ Changes the steppe vegetation. When burrowing, it brings subsoil to the surface, in which different plants can grow.
○ Droppings fertilise the soil.
○ Hibernates in burrows.

Pine marten

○ Agile pine forest dweller.
○ Large paws and sharp claws help it grip branches and it uses its long, bushy tail for balancing.
○ Catches squirrels and birds in the trees, and rabbits, rodents and insects on the ground. It also forages for berries.
○ Marks a path through the trees with scent from a gland under its tail.

Onager

○ Also called wild ass, runs as fast as a racehorse, at around 65 km/h.
○ Can survive harsh desert climate for two or three days without drinking.
○ Greatest enemy is humans, but it lives in barren places where few people go.
○ In summer, it eats upland grasses. In winter, the cold and lack of pasture drive it south.

Mongolian gerbil

○ During the day, the gerbil shelters in its burrow from the intense desert heat.
○ Most active just before sunset, when it comes out in search of grasses and seeds.
○ Never needs to drink and doesn't sweat.
○ Kidneys are adapted to produce small amounts of concentrated urine, so it doesn't waste any water.

Freshwater seal

Lake Baikal in Russia is the oldest and deepest lake in the world, and three-quarters of its animals are found nowhere else on Earth. The *Baikal seal,* the only seal found in fresh water, probably arrived in the lake when the glaciers melted at the end of the last Ice Age. During the last century, the numbers of Baikal seals were severely reduced by hunting. Recent conservation measures have led to a slight recovery.

Feather cushion

The male *great bustard* puts on an extraordinary display to attract a mate. He gulps in air to inflate a sac in his throat, which balloons out until his head is thrust back and he seems to turn inside out in a flurry of white feathers. The male mates with four or five females, who incubate the eggs in a shallow scrape nest and rear the chicks alone, feeding them by beak until they learn to peck the grass seeds of the steppe and to eat insects.

HIMALAYAS AND CHINA

ASIA

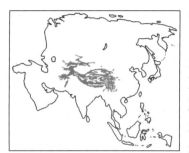

The Himalayas form the great mountain system of Asia that separates the cold north from the tropical south. The twin ranges extend over 2,400 km, from Pakistan across northern India to Bhutan. The highest peaks in the world, including Mount Everest at 8,848 m, are found here. While much of Asia is dry, parts of the Himalayas receive the world's highest rainfall. On the snow-capped peaks, where it is bitterly cold and blizzards are commonplace, nothing can survive. But the crags and valleys at lower altitudes provide a mix of habitats for a wide range of animals.

In the foothills, tropical forests teem with insects, frogs, lizards, snakes, birds and mammals. Higher up, the tropical trees give way to forests of rhododendrons and bamboo that echo to the musical song of the hill mynah. Above the tree line, grassy meadows are filled with flowers in summer, providing food for butterflies such as the apollo. The snow leopard hunts here for ibex and other prey. Only the yak, with its thick coat, can remain at high altitudes through the coldest months.

The mountains of the east continue into western and central China, covering about one-third of its area. Arctic winds make it bitterly cold in winter, while in summer it is warm and dry. In the misty mountain forests, the giant panda strips bamboo shoots, its only source of food.

Peaceful giant

Giant pandas live alone in the mountain bamboo forests of southwestern China. The bamboo is so low in nutrients that they need to eat for 16 hours a day. Every 50 years or so, large areas of bamboo flower, seed and die. Because pandas cannot migrate across farmland or areas of human habitation, sanctuaries are being set up by Chinese conservationists.

Flashy courtship

The male *golden pheasant* uses his colourful plumage to attract a female during the mating season. He turns the bright feathers round his neck forwards to cover his beak like a fan. Golden pheasants build their nests on the ground in the forests of central China. The female incubates the eggs and rears the young alone. The chicks can feed as soon as they hatch, and fly a week later.

Thick fur

The *snow leopard* lives high in the Himalayas. It preys on sheep, goats and deer above the tree line in summer. In winter, it follows its prey down to the valleys, where it finds gazelle and wild boar. The hairy pads under its paws help it leap across the snow without sinking. Its beautiful thick pelt is sought after by fur trappers who have greatly reduced its numbers.

Brown wings

The *apollo butterfly* sips nectar from the short, hardy plants that bloom in the Himalayas in spring. Its drab colours help it to survive the harsh mountain climate – the browns of its wings absorb heat, allowing it to warm up quickly in the Sun. Dark colours also shut out the Sun's ultraviolet rays (which are stronger in the thin mountain air). Many small mountain creatures have dark colouring for this reason.

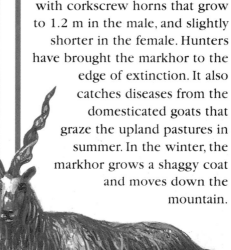

Twisted horns

The *markhor* is a Himalayan goat with corkscrew horns that grow to 1.2 m in the male, and slightly shorter in the female. Hunters have brought the markhor to the edge of extinction. It also catches diseases from the domesticated goats that graze the upland pastures in summer. In the winter, the markhor grows a shaggy coat and moves down the mountain.

Brilliant mimic

The chattering of the *hill mynah* can be heard in the tropical forests and plantations of the Himalayas and southern China. It lives in small flocks, foraging for fruit and berries, catching insects such as the winged termite and sipping nectar from flowering trees. Its strong legs and feet are better adapted to perching than to hopping on the ground. In captivity, the hill mynah can accurately mimic human speech.

Domesticated yaks

Yaks are cattle that live on the high Tibetan plain. Their long, shaggy coat protects them from the cold, and they are sure-footed enough to cope with the rough terrain. Wild yaks have been hunted almost to extinction, but domesticated yaks are essential for the survival of the mountain people. They provide milk, meat, hides and wool, and are used as pack animals and to pull carts.

TROPICAL FORESTS

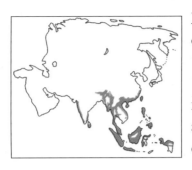

Much of Southeast Asia is covered with a dense green carpet of tropical forest that is warm and wet all year round. About 100 square km of forest can contain over 400 species of bird, 100 different reptile species and uncountable species of insect. Tropical forest trees can reach heights of over 30 m, and within the forest there are several layers, each with its own characteristic animals.

Above the tree tops, insect-eating bats and birds, such as nightjars, dart and swerve to catch flying insects. Below them is the canopy. Birds, such as hornbills, and fruit bats feed on fruit and flowers. Monkeys and squirrels scamper along branches in search of leaves, fruit and insects, keeping a wary eye out for birds of prey, such as serpent eagles. Gibbons swing gracefully through the branches.

Below this, in the understorey, hordes of insects travel up and down the tree trunks and creepers, called lianas. The insects are prey for lizards and tree frogs, both of which are ideal food for tree snakes. Little light gets through to the forest floor, but plenty of food falls from the canopy above for foraging pigs and tapirs. These are prey for large predators, such as tigers, as are the smaller insect-eating mammals.

Flexible snout

A shy, nocturnal (night) creature that scurries along well-worn tracks, the *Malay tapir* lives deep in the tropical forests of Southeast Asia. It uses its long, flexible snout and upper lip like an elephant uses its trunk – to pluck grasses, leaves, buds and fruit. If surprised by an enemy, the tapir may dive into a swamp to escape. It is a strong swimmer and also eats water plants.

Toddy cat

A night-hunter, the solitary *palm civet* rests in the tree tops during the day. It moves stealthily, well camouflaged by its markings, then ambushes its prey. It feeds on small mammals, insects and fruit and is sometimes called the toddy cat, because it raids palm plantations and steals fermenting palm juice used to make toddy, the local alcoholic drink.

Is it a leaf?

The *Asian horned frog* is camouflaged to look like the dead leaves that are found on the forest floor. It has three 'leaf points', or horns, one over each eye and one above its mouth, and 'leaf ribs' on its skin. Its brilliant disguise hides it from predators and prey. The male advertises his presence only in the mating season, when he calls loudly. He risks his life so the female can find him.

Cock of the roost

The male *red junglefowl* is the ancestor of the domestic cockerel, which it looks like. Small groups live at the edge of the rainforest, scratching for roots, seeds and insects. In spring, the male displays his colourful plumage, then mates with several females. The hens lay their eggs in nests deeply hidden in the undergrowth. Chicks hatch in around three weeks.

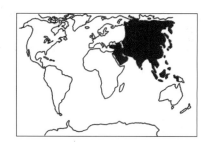

Swinging ape

The *gibbon*'s long, muscular arms and strong fingers allow it to move by brachiating – swinging arm over arm along the branches. Its shoulder and wrist joints are very mobile, so it can turn right round while hanging by one hand. Gibbons feed on fruit, young leaves and flowers. At dawn and dusk, they call to each other and to neighbouring groups. The female leads a duet with her mate. The baby clings to its mother's fur as she travels, and feeds on her milk for up to two years.

Project Tiger

In 1900, there were around 40,000 *tigers* in India, but 70 years later, big game hunting and loss of habitat to farmland had reduced the numbers to only 1,800. Project Tiger was set up in 1973. Villagers were rehoused to provide room for tiger sanctuaries. Within ten years, the tiger population had risen to 3,000. Today, work continues to resolve the problem of farmers taking over the tiger's territory and of tigers killing farmers' livestock.

Snake-eater

The *king cobra* is the largest venomous snake in the world, over 5 m in length. When aroused, it rears up and spreads the ribs and loose skin at the side of its head to make a hood. Its main prey is other snakes. The female lays a clutch of 20 to 40 eggs in a nest of leaves on the forest floor and guards them until they hatch.

INDONESIA

ASIA

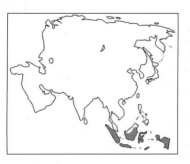

Located in Southeast Asia, Indonesia is a massive group of over 13,000 islands, covering 2 million square km and stretching across 8 million square km of the Indian Ocean. The main islands include Sumatra, Java, Sulawesi, Kalimantan (part of Borneo) and Irian Jaya (part of New Guinea). Indonesia's islands are mountainous and dotted with volcanoes, some of them active. The climate is tropical with plenty of rainfall.

Over two-thirds of Indonesia's landscape is covered by tropical forest, and nearly 10 per cent of the world's rainforests are found here. The forests contain a huge array of animal life. The orang-utan feeds on fruit, and Asian elephants and rhinoceroses trundle through the undergrowth, browsing on leaves and branches. Tigers use their striped coat as camouflage to conceal themselves as they stalk unwary prey. A deer darts through the trees, only to be caught by the fearsome Komodo dragon.

Today, uncontrolled logging and the spread of agriculture is tearing the heart out of these forests and threatening many of the animals. As trees disappear, topsoil is washed into the sea, clogging and destroying Indonesia's coral reefs, which are rich in marine life. Indonesia also has vast stretches of mangrove swamps that are rich breeding grounds for fish.

Long arms

The *orang-utan* is a shy, solitary ape. The male, which is much larger than the female, stakes out his territory in the forest and mates with several females, who look after their offspring for around three years. At night, orang-utans construct a sleeping platform of branches in the tree tops. Their habitat is now under threat and orang-utan mothers are often killed and their babies put in zoos.

Horned nose

The two-horned *Sumatran rhinoceros* uses its prehensile (grasping) upper lip for tearing at shrubs. The young rhinos have a shaggy coat, but lose it as they grow. The adults have little hair to protect them against the Sun, so they often wallow in water or mud to cool down. The Sumatran rhino's only enemies are humans and other rhinos – males charge at each other and clash horns.

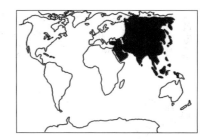

Orange horn

Its huge beak allows the *rhinoceros hornbill* to reach fruit growing on the end of slender twigs. The bill is hollow for lightness and strengthened with bony struts. On top of it is a massive 'rhinoceros horn' called a casque, which is used for display and to show the bird's status. A strong flier, it lives high in the rainforest canopy and nests in a hole in a tree, plastering over the entrance to leave just a small feeding hole.

Land-fish

The *mudskipper* lives mostly on land, skipping over the mud in mangrove swamps on its muscular pectoral fins. It breathes by keeping water inside the large cavity around its gills. It shelters in a burrow. Its eyes move independently of one another, searching for crustaceans, insects and worms. In the mating season, the male develops brighter colours on its back.

Meat-eating bat

Most bats feed on insects, but the *greater false vampire bat* also preys on small mammals, lizards, frogs, birds and other bats. It hunts at night, using sight as well as echolocation to find its prey, flying low among trees and undergrowth. The false vampire bites its prey on the back of the neck to kill it, then flies off with it to its roost to feed.

Slash and burn

Indonesia's tropical forests have come under increasing threat as its population has increased and people need more land to grow crops. As the forests disappear, animals such as the orang-utan, found only here, face a difficult future. Forest destruction often takes the form of 'slash and burn' – ruthless cutting down of trees and burning vegetation. In the late 1990s, this produced appalling smoke pollution that affected people's health throughout Southeast Asia.

Huge lizard

At 3 m long, the *Komodo dragon* is the largest land lizard that has ever lived. It can eat a whole deer in one meal, then rest for a week to digest it. Despite their size, Komodo dragons move fast and will eat almost any animal on the hilly forested islands where they live, including other dragons. The males fight to defend their territory and to attract a mate. Baby dragons hatch, fully formed, from large, leathery eggs.

AFRICA

Africa is the world's second largest continent. In the north are the great wastes of the Sahara desert, which covers 9 million square km – an area as big as the United States. Here, the addax, desert hedgehog and sandgrouse survive under the fierce Sun. At the steamy heart of Africa, tropical rainforest stretches from the Gulf of Guinea in the west across the Congo Basin. The hot, wet environment produces extremes of size, seen in the tiny royal antelope and the enormous goliath beetle, and richly coloured birds, such as the Congo peafowl.

The rainforest gives way to savanna – vast expanses of open grassland dotted with trees and scrubby bushes. The savanna is home to the world's largest herds of grazing animals, as well as the big cats, scavenging dogs and vultures.

East Africa is dominated by the Great Rift Valley – huge cracks in the Earth's crust that have flooded in parts to form a chain of long, deep lakes. Crocodiles lurk in the shallows and spectacular flocks of pink flamingoes feed on algae and tiny shrimps. Eagles soar over the mountain ranges while baboons and the rare ibex leap from crag to crag. In the swamplands that dot the continent, hippos wallow.

Desert

The *meerkat* is a rabbit-sized animal that lives in the deserts and dry areas of southern Africa. These sociable relatives of the mongoose live in groups and share the work. At daybreak, they warm themselves in the Sun while one animal acts as a sentry to watch out for enemies such as eagles. Some babysit the young, and the rest go hunting for lizards, ground-nesting birds and rodents. Meerkats can kill and eat dangerous prey – they are immune to scorpion and snakebite venom (which would kill a human). At dusk, they take refuge in a network of burrows.

Savanna

The *impala* is a grass-eater that migrates in herds across the savanna. Its markings break up its outline, which confuses predators as the herd swirls and turns to evade them. In the breeding season, the males fight each other for territory in light scrubland that will provide cover for the young. They lock horns in an attempt to throw each other to the ground. (The winner may hold the territory for only a few days until the next rival comes along.) In early summer, when vegetation is at its richest, the females bear a single calf. The young are watched over by their mother until they are strong enough to run with the herd.

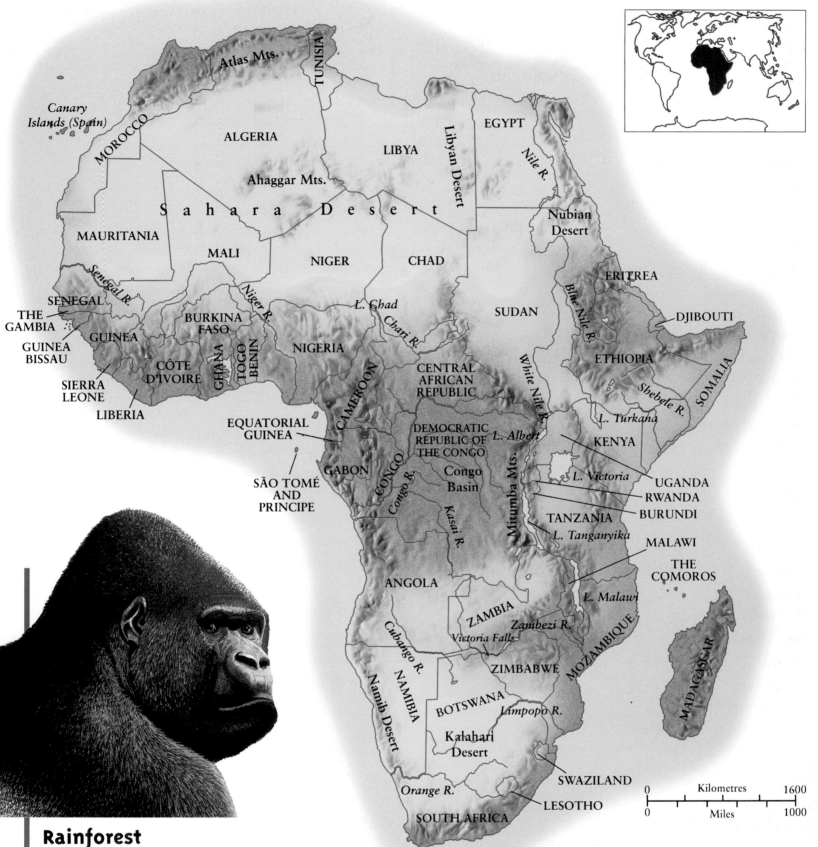

Canary Islands (Spain)

MOROCCO
Atlas Mts.
TUNISIA
ALGERIA
LIBYA
Libyan Desert
EGYPT
Nile R.
Ahaggar Mts.
S a h a r a   D e s e r t
Nubian Desert
MAURITANIA
MALI
NIGER
CHAD
SUDAN
ERITREA
Senegal R.
Niger R.
L. Chad
Chari R.
Blue Nile R.
DJIBOUTI
SENEGAL
THE GAMBIA
GUINEA BISSAU
GUINEA
BURKINA FASO
BENIN
NIGERIA
White Nile R.
ETHIOPIA
Shebele R.
SOMALIA
SIERRA LEONE
LIBERIA
CÔTE D'IVOIRE
GHANA
TOGO
CENTRAL AFRICAN REPUBLIC
L. Turkana
EQUATORIAL GUINEA
CAMEROON
DEMOCRATIC REPUBLIC OF THE CONGO
L. Albert
KENYA
GABON
CONGO
Congo R.
Congo Basin
Mitumba Mts.
L. Victoria
UGANDA
RWANDA
BURUNDI
SÃO TOMÉ AND PRINCIPE
Kasai R.
TANZANIA
L. Tanganyika
MALAWI
THE COMOROS
ANGOLA
L. Malawi
Cubango R.
ZAMBIA
Zambezi R.
MOZAMBIQUE
Victoria Falls
MADAGASCAR
Namib Desert
NAMIBIA
ZIMBABWE
BOTSWANA
Limpopo R.
Kalahari Desert
Orange R.
SWAZILAND
LESOTHO
SOUTH AFRICA

| 0 | Kilometres | 1600 |
| 0 | Miles | 1000 |

Rainforest

Gorillas are the world's largest apes. They live in family groups and feed on leaves, shoots and stems. A mature male, known as a silverback because of the colour of his hair, leads the group. Up to 16 years old, weighing around 200 kg, silverbacks are too heavy to be tree-dwellers. The females and their young may climb into the trees to feed and sleep. If challenged by a young male, a silverback will roar and beat his chest, but gorillas are rarely aggressive. Because of hunting and the destruction of their forest habitat, fewer than 1,000 gorillas remain.

Swamps and lakes

The *Nile crocodile* was once found all over Africa. It preys on wildebeest, gazelle, buffalo and lions, and will also eat people. The crocodile ambushes its prey, then drags it underwater to drown it. It stores the dead creature underwater until it begins to rot. The crocodile cannot chew, but tears off huge chunks of flesh and gulps them down. It eats every scrap, digesting everything with stones it has swallowed to grind the food in its stomach.

37

SAVANNA

AFRICA

The African savanna is one of the last great natural grasslands on Earth. It is home to many of the world's largest land mammals, both plant-eaters (herbivores) and their predators (carnivores). The grasses are heavily cropped by large herds of herbivores such as zebras and gazelles. New shoots appear as taller stalks are nibbled off. Each species feeds on a different part of the grass, so they do not compete with one another. Other herbivores are browsers: rhinos eat scrubby twigs, while elephants and giraffes pluck leaves from tall trees.

Many grazers and browsers are the food of lions, leopards and wild dogs. After the killers have feasted, vultures and other scavengers, such as hyenas, move in. Within hours, the bones are picked bare, and carrion flies and beetles can finish the job.

The savanna has two seasons, hot and wet and hot and dry. As the grasses become parched, the herds move to fresh grazing lands. When the warm rains come, the land turns green. Within a few days during the wet season, all the females of a grazing herd give birth. This means that, although their predators have a feast, as many young as possible survive.

Striped horse

For most of the year, *zebras* live in scattered groups of 10 to 15 animals, usually one male and the rest females and their foals. In the dry season, they mass into large herds that stretch as far as the eye can see. There is safety in numbers, but as zebras gallop across the savanna, some fall prey to predators such as lions, wild dogs and hyenas.

Tender mother

The *scorpion* hunts at night by detecting the vibrations of its prey. It grabs its victim with its pincers, sometimes using its sting to paralyse it. The sting of some scorpions can kill large animals and people. A scorpion lays about 100 eggs. When they hatch, the young climb onto their mother's back until they are able to fend for themselves.

Endangered rhino

The *black rhino* has been hunted to the verge of extinction for its nose horn, which poachers sell to be carved into dagger handles and crushed to make traditional medicines. Some people still believe it has mysterious powers, but rhino horn is actually made of keratin, the same material that forms human hair and nails. Some conservationists have tried to save black rhinos by sawing off their horns before they fall victim to poachers. This is a painless process for the rhinos.

Ostrich

○ World's largest bird.
○ Can't fly but can run faster than any other animal on two legs, sprinting up to 70 km/h.
○ Only bird in the world with just two toes on its foot. It has very sharp claws and can give a deadly kick in self-defence.
○ Lays the largest eggs, each 20 times as big as a hen's egg.
○ Males and females pair up to breed, sharing nest duty. But other females also lay in the nest, so the birds sit on up to 40 eggs.

African hunting dog

○ Also called the African wild dog, lives in packs of between 6 and 20 animals.
○ Rests during the day and hunts at dawn and dusk.
○ Prey includes zebra and impala. Returns to the den to disgorge food for the dogs that stayed behind with the young.
○ Very social animals, sharing care for the young, old and sick in the pack.
○ Nomadic, settling down for three months of the year, when the pups are born in an underground den.

Wildebeest

○ Herds roam thousands of kilometres across the savanna in search of grass.
○ When they graze, they protect their young by surrounding them.
○ Give birth standing up. The baby gets to its feet immediately and can run with the herd in a few hours.
○ Herds of wildebeest and zebra often merge to provide greater protection against prowling predators like lions.

Secretary bird

○ A bird of prey that does not swoop but stomps on its prey to kill it, then tears it apart using its beak.
○ Can be 1.2 m tall, wings can span 2 m.
○ Soars in the air like other birds of prey, but spends most of its time walking.
○ Pairs for life, sleeping with its mate in their nest all year round.
○ Feeds on rodents, insects and snakes, regurgitating its prey for its young.

Top cat

Lions live in a pride of 20 to 30 animals. Each pride has up to four males, distinguished by their manes. Male cubs are driven from the pride at two years old. Rival lions often fight to the death. The lionesses do most of the work, sharing cub-care and hunting in an organised group while the males rest. When they kill an animal, they may wait until the male has eaten before feeding themselves.

Intelligent giant

African elephants are the world's largest land animals. Calves are suckled by their mother for two years, then between the ages of 8 and 20, the young bulls are driven from the herd and form a separate bachelor group. An elephant rips leaves from the trees with its trunk and tusks and uses its trunk, an extension of its upper lip and nose, as a 'hand' to feed itself.

TROPICAL RAINFOREST

The African rainforest stretches from the west coast to the Rift Valley. Wildlife thrives in this permanently warm, humid, evergreen environment. Tall emergent trees push through the forest canopy. In clearings where a tree has fallen, saplings thrust up towards the light. Monkeys swing through the trees and crowned eagles soar, looking for birds and squirrels. Pythons coil round branches, chimps and gorillas eat leaves and fruit, and butterflies flit through the air. Antelopes browse on bushes, wild pigs, porcupines and termites eat leaves and rotting fruit, and pygmy hippos bathe in swamps.

There is plenty to eat in the tropical rainforests and some species grow extra large. The African giant snail is the biggest in the world – its shell is 25 cm across, almost the size of a soccer ball. The goliath frog swallows mice whole and the praying mantis can kill small lizards. Camouflage is important in the densely populated forest. Predators such as leopards are difficult to spot in dappled shade. The splashy markings on genets (cat-like hunters) and antelopes make them almost invisible as rays of light fall on the dark undergrowth. There are green tree snakes and some moths that look like leaves.

Chatterbox

The *grey parrot* screeches and whistles in the rainforest, where it feeds on seeds, nuts and fruit. It roosts in the tree tops at night and makes a nest in a tree hole in the breeding season. Two of the parrot's toes point forwards and two backwards, which makes it easy for it to clamber in trees, using its hooked beak as a 'third foot'. It also uses its foot to grip food. Because it is a good mimic and can be taught to 'talk', the grey parrot is at risk from poachers, who sell birds to the pet trade.

Armour-plated

The *pangolin* lives in the trees and moves from branch to branch, grasping the bark with its feet and its prehensile tail, which grips like an extra foot. Its skin is covered with scales that overlap and help to protect it from predators. When attacked, it rolls into a ball, safe from all but hyenas and the largest cats. The pangolin eats termites and ants. It uses its claws to rip into a nest, sweeping them up with flicks of its long tongue.

Spotted hunter

The *leopard* is a solitary member of the cat family that marks out its territory with claw marks and urine. It often hunts near water, waiting in a tree for its prey to come to drink. It eats fish, birds, snakes, monkeys, okapi and antelope, dragging its kill into a tree, where scavengers can't steal it. This provides the leopard with food for several days.

Hungry bride

The *praying mantis* gets its name from the way it waits, motionless, as if in prayer. It turns its head as it waits for an insect to come into range, then shoots out its arms to grab it. The mantis scoops out the juicy bits of its prey with its mouthparts, leaving the tough shell, wings and legs. The female is larger than the male and often eats her partner while they are mating.

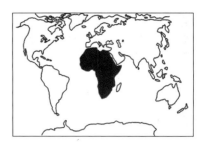

Clever chimp

Chimpanzees live in troops of 15 to 80 animals. They eat fruit, leaves, insects, grubs and honey. Sometimes they kill larger animals, such as monkeys. At night, chimps sleep in a nest they make in the trees. The young travel on their mother's back. They are weaned at about four years old, but remain dependent for several more years. The chimp is a highly intelligent animal, and can use sticks as tools.

Deadly fangs

The venomous *gaboon viper* can be 2 m long. Its fangs are the longest of any snake (up to 5 cm) and one bite could kill a human. It hides on the forest floor, where its markings in buff, purple, pink and brown provide excellent camouflage among the leaf litter. It eats frogs, birds and rodents. It can give birth to 60 live young, which are able to fend for themselves as soon as they are born.

Honey lovers

The *ratel*, also known as the honey badger, often teams up with a bird called a *honeyguide*. To attract the ratel's attention, the honeyguide flicks its tail and makes a loud chattering noise. Then the bird leads the ratel to a bees' nest. The ratel breaks open the nest with its claws as the bird looks on, then both creatures eat the honey and grubs inside.

41

DESERTS

AFRICA

The Sahara is the largest desert on Earth. The scorching Sun beats down by day, but at night it gets extremely cold and it hardly ever rains. One-tenth of the Sahara is made up of sand dunes, the rest is rock, silt and gravel. But few parts of the desert are completely barren. Tough grasses and spiny bushes grow in the stony wastelands. Other plants have fleshy leaves and stalks that absorb the heavy dew. When rain falls, seeds sprout after lying dormant for months or years, and the desert floor is carpeted briefly with flowers.

The creatures that live in the Sahara and Africa's southern deserts, the Kalahari and the Namib, have adapted to survive harsh conditions. Insects, scorpions and spiders have a hard, shiny skin to stop their body drying out. Reptiles such as snakes and lizards need the Sun's warmth to make them active. Some animals, like the sand cat, have thick fur under their feet to protect them against the burning ground. The lack of water is the greatest challenge to survival. Many animals, like the barbary sheep, get all the moisture they need from eating plants. Desert mammals hardly sweat at all and their urine is concentrated, so they do not lose excess water.

High jump

The *desert jerboa* is a small rodent like a tiny kangaroo. Its strong back legs are four times as long as its front legs, and it can jump up to 2.5 m to escape from its predators. Its long tail helps it to balance. The jerboa uses its short arms for burrowing in the desert sand. During the day, it rests in its burrow, coming out at dusk to eat insects and seeds. Plants provide all the moisture the jerboa needs, so it never has to drink.

Tiny fox

The *fennec fox* is the smallest of the foxes, and grows to only 40 cm. Its huge ears, 15 cm long, act like a radiator to give off heat and help the animal keep cool. They also provide the fennec fox with excellent hearing. It hunts mainly by sound, listening out for termites and other insects, lizards and jerboas. By day, it rests and shelters from the fierce heat in its burrow.

Snakes and ladders

The *desert horned viper* moves across the loose sand in an unusual way, leaving telltale 'ladder' tracks. It burrows by wriggling until it has disappeared into the sand, leaving only its eyes and nostrils peeping out to watch for prey or danger. It hunts mainly at night, feeding on small creatures such as lizards.

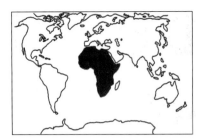

Spiny tail

Reptiles control their body temperature by gaining or losing heat from the environment. They need less energy and food than warm-blooded creatures, which have to generate heat in their own body. The *dabb spiny-tailed lizard* stores fat in its spiny tail. It can live on this if it finds no insects or plants to eat. It also uses the spines on its tail to defend itself against enemies.

Rare survivor

The *addax* can survive extreme heat and drought. Its wide hooves stop it sinking into the sand as it searches for the scant desert vegetation. It gets all its moisture from grasses and leaves and never needs to drink. A shy creature, it has been hunted(for its skin and meat) and is now very rare.

Desert cleaner

Dung beetles clean up the desert by eating the droppings of other animals. They roll the dung into marble-sized balls, then trundle them to their nests, pushing the balls along with their back legs. At their nesting site, they bury the dung balls, first laying an egg in each one. In this way, the hatching beetles are provided with a good supply of nutritious food.

Ship of the desert

The *dromedary*, or Arabian camel, has a single hump. This is made up mainly of fat, to keep the camel going. The camel can survive for weeks without food or drink, but when it gets to water, it will gulp up to 50 litres in a few minutes. In sandstorms, its long, thick eyelashes protect its eyes, and it can close its nostrils. Camels can travel up to 50 km a day. Their swaying walk has earned them the affectionate nickname 'ship of the desert'.

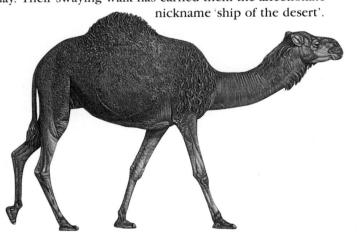

WETLANDS AND MOUNTAINS

AFRICA

Africa's wetlands include the great lakes of the eastern Rift Valley, the swamps and flood plains of the Okavango delta in Botswana and the Kafue flood plain in Zambia. Wetlands are packed with animal life, as well as fish like the Nile perch. Wetland antelopes, such as the lechwe, feed on the lush vegetation and seek refuge in the water if a predator appears. Hippos need water to shelter them from the fierce Sun during the day. Water birds feed in the wetlands, and many stop off there while migrating. Crocodiles lurk in the swamps, ready to snap up passing prey.

To the east of equatorial Africa lie several mountain ranges. The single highest peak, at almost 6,000 m, is Mount Kilimanjaro. These mountains are tropical and are exposed to hot, intense sunshine during the day and freezing cold nights. The mountains are rich in animal life, which changes with increasing altitude. At the lowest level is savanna grassland. Higher up are montane forests of cedar and camphor trees and, higher still, bamboo forests. The forests and clearings are home to many birds, such as parrots, and large mammals, including black rhinos and elephants, primates such as bushbabies and predators such as lions. Few large animals venture above the tree line to the high alpine meadows and heathlands. Here rodents and hyraxes live, always watchful of danger from eagles. Unusual alpine plants grow here, like the giant lobelia that provides food for the scarlet tufted malachite sunbird. At the top, the bare rock and snow provide no shelter for wildlife.

WETLANDS
Daytime wallowers

The heavyweight *hippopotamus* wallows in the muddy waters of lakes and rivers to cool off in the heat of the day and avoid burning its hairless skin. Being in water in a herd provides extra protection for young hippos from enemies. Male hippos compete for mates by opening their mouth wide to show off their massive tusks. Despite their large size, hippos are excellent swimmers and divers. At night, they leave the water and follow well-worn paths to 'hippo meadows', where they graze on grasses until dawn.

Swimming antelope

The *lechwe* is an antelope that lives in lake and riverside marshes. Lechwes are sociable animals that wade in the water, grazing on water plants and grass. If threatened by a cheetah or lion, they quickly leap through the water. They are good swimmers, and can go underwater with just their nostrils showing. Lechwes only really go onto dry land to rest and give birth.

Lily trotter

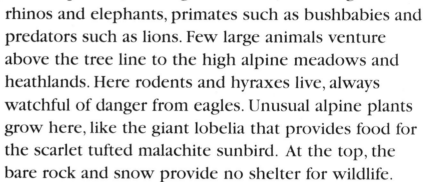

The long-toed spreading feet of the *African jacana* allow it to walk over lily pads and other water plants without sinking, giving it its other name, the lily trotter. The jacana feeds on insects and crustaceans. If threatened, it hides underwater with only its bill and nostrils showing. The male makes a floating nest for his mate, and incubates the eggs and rears the chicks himself.

MOUNTAINS
Sun-lovers

The sociable, rabbit-sized *rock hyrax* makes its home in caves on rocky outcrops, where up to 100 live together, emerging in the morning to warm up in the Sun. They survive on very little water and crop plants with their cheek teeth. They bare their long incisors (front teeth) in self-defence. Their feet have rubbery soles which give a good grip for climbing.

Rare feast

The long-beaked *scarlet tufted malachite sunbird* sips nectar from lobelia flowers. As it feeds, it gets brushed with pollen and this fertilises the next lobelia it visits. Unlike a hummingbird, it perches instead of hovers and it eats insects. To attract a female, the male displays his red tuft and shivers his wings. The pair build a nest stuck together with spiders' webs.

Big hair

The *gelada* is a mountain-dwelling baboon. The male has a thick mane hanging down his back. The bare patch of red skin on his chest expands when he is frightened or angry. Each male heads a group of about 12 females and their young. During the day, geladas descend to the grasslands to feed, returning to the mountains at dusk to sleep on a rocky ledge.

Feet first

Soaring on updraughts of warm air, *Verreaux's eagle* scours the mountains with its sharp eyes for rabbits and rock hyraxes. Then it swoops down, kills its prey with a heavy blow from its foot, and grips it in its talons. In the breeding season, Verreaux's eagles take their catch to the nest to feed to their young. They also feed on the carcasses of animals that have slipped and fallen to their death.

Upsetting the balance

Lake Victoria in East Africa was once home to 300 species of *cichlid* fish. Cichlids are unusual in that they brood their young in their mouth. In the 1960s, Nile perch were introduced into the lake as a catch for fishermen. The perch fed on the cichlids and multiplied rapidly, providing local people with plenty to eat. But the cichlids declined, and now at least 200 of the species are extinct.

45

NORTH AMERICA

North America is the world's third largest continent with an area of some 24.4 million square km and a huge range of habitats. Despite the destruction of some of the continent's wild places for industrial development, building and agriculture, these habitats still contain a vast variety of animal life. North America stretches from the cold polar regions of northern Canada in the north, to the tropical forests of Central America in the south, and is bordered by the mighty Pacific Ocean in the west and the Atlantic in the east.

Two mountain chains dominate the continent. The high Rockies run down the west side, while the Appalachians rise in the east. Hardy sheep and goats can survive the harsh mountain conditions, as can their predators, the bobcat and lynx. Stretched out between the two mountain chains are the fertile Great Plains, once prairie grassland but now mainly agricultural land. A broad band of coniferous forests covers much of the north, as well as the slopes of the Rockies. Vast broad-leaved forests of maples and oaks grow south of the Great Lakes and on both sides of the Appalachians. In spring and summer, these are filled with insects, birds and mammals. Warm wetlands in the southeast form an ideal habitat for water birds and alligators. By contrast, the southwest is a dry area of deserts, where many animals seek shade during the day and emerge to feed at night.

Forests

The *Virginia opossum* is North America's only marsupial. Like the kangaroo, it has a pouch on its belly into which the tiny, underdeveloped young are born. The cat-sized opossum has a litter of up to 20 young, but only the strongest survive, as the mother does not have enough nipples in her pouch to feed them all. It nests on the ground and forages in leaf litter on the forest floor and in trees for its food, such as insects, fruit and small mammals. It is a good climber with strong claws for gripping and a prehensile tail, which it twines round branches to serve as a fifth limb.

Mountains

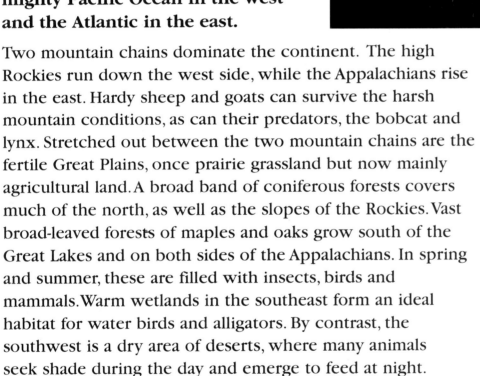

The *mountain bluebird* is a kind of thrush. It is found in open meadowland dotted with trees high in the Rockies. The male has beautiful blue plumage, while the female is a duller grey-brown. They make their nest in a tree hole and rear about five chicks. In summer, the mountain bluebird lives above 1,500 m, feeding on insects caught on the wing. In winter, bluebirds move down the mountains and gather in flocks to feed on fruit. Some migrate south to Mexico.

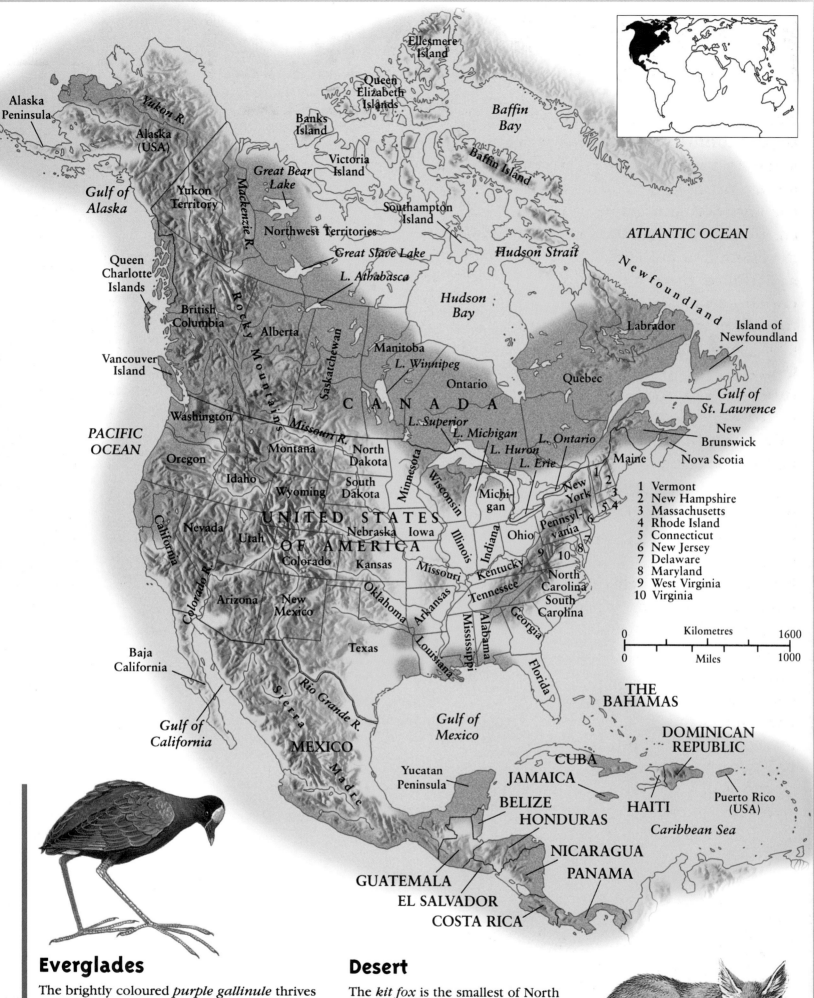

Alaska
Peninsula

Alaska
(USA)

Yukon R.

Gulf of
Alaska

Yukon
Territory

Queen
Charlotte
Islands

British
Columbia

Vancouver
Island

Washington

PACIFIC
OCEAN

Oregon

Idaho

Nevada

California

Utah

Baja
California

Gulf of
California

Ellesmere
Island

Queen
Elizabeth
Islands

Banks
Island

Victoria
Island

Baffin
Bay

Baffin Island

Great Bear
Lake

Mackenzie R.

Northwest Territories

Southampton
Island

Great Slave Lake

L. Athabasca

Rocky Mountains

Alberta

Saskatchewan

Manitoba

L. Winnipeg

Missouri R.

Montana

North
Dakota

Wyoming

South
Dakota

Minnesota

Hudson Strait

Hudson
Bay

Ontario

CANADA

L. Superior

Wisconsin

L. Michigan

Michi-
gan

L. Huron

L. Ontario

Quebec

L. Erie

ATLANTIC OCEAN

Newfoundland

Labrador

Island of
Newfoundland

Gulf of
St. Lawrence

New
Brunswick

Nova Scotia

Maine

1 Vermont
2 New Hampshire
3 Massachusetts
4 Rhode Island
5 Connecticut
6 New Jersey
7 Delaware
8 Maryland
9 West Virginia
10 Virginia

UNITED STATES
OF AMERICA

Nebraska

Iowa

Colorado

Kansas

Illinois

Indiana

Ohio

New
York

Pennsyl-
vania

Missouri

Kentucky

Arizona

New
Mexico

Oklahoma

Arkansas

Tennessee

North
Carolina

South
Carolina

Colorado R.

Sierra

Rio Grande R.

Texas

Louisiana

Mississippi

Alabama

Georgia

Florida

MEXICO

Madre

Yucatan
Peninsula

Gulf of
Mexico

THE
BAHAMAS

CUBA

JAMAICA

BELIZE

HONDURAS

NICARAGUA

GUATEMALA

PANAMA

EL SALVADOR

COSTA RICA

HAITI

DOMINICAN
REPUBLIC

Puerto Rico
(USA)

Caribbean Sea

Kilometres
0   1600

Miles
0   1000

Everglades

The brightly coloured *purple gallinule* thrives in the lush, warm swamplands of the Florida Everglades. Its long, spreading toes allow it to walk easily over lily pads and other floating plants, searching for small fish, frogs and insects. It is also an agile climber. It hops up reeds and rice plants to eat the seeds, and feeds on berries in bushes. It builds a cup-shaped nest close to the water.

Desert

The *kit fox* is the smallest of North America's foxes and lives in the arid wastelands of the western deserts. It hunts at night, using its large ears and good hearing to locate lizards, rodents and rabbits. It approaches stealthily, then leaps in the air and lands on its prey, squashing it with its front paws. Solitary for most of the year, the foxes share the job of parenting. Cubs are born in a den, and both parents bring them food once they are weaned.

47

NORTH AMERICA

Coniferous forests of spruce, pine, larch and fir stretch for almost 6,400 km, from Alaska and across most of Canada, broken only by lakes and rivers. Here, the summers are warm, but the winters are bitterly cold. The lynx and its main prey, the snowshoe hare, have thickly furred feet to stop them sinking into deep snow. The short summer sees the arrival of insect-eating birds to breed, and the departure of the caribou (reindeer) to the colder, treeless tundra further north. Birds of prey feed on rodents that are plentiful in summer.

Forests
Woodlands

The woodlands south of the Great Lakes and on both sides of the Appalachian mountains in Canada and the USA are filled with over 150 species of deciduous, broad-leaved trees, including maple, oak and beech. These provide a rich habitat for many animals. As the spring sunlight warms the forest floor, wild flowers spring up and the trees start to regain their leaves. The flowers provide food for insects and rodents. Many birds – both new arrivals from winter homes and year-round residents – feed on insects as they build their nests and breed. Hawks and owls, as well as raccoons and opossums thrive. In autumn, the leaves turn red and gold before they fall.

Champion migrant

In autumn, millions of *monarch butterflies* set off from Canada and northern USA on a huge migration to California and Mexico. Here, they hibernate in winter roosting sites, completely covering the trees. In spring, they awake and flutter to the ground to sip nectar from milkweed flowers. Then they begin flying north. During the journey, many mate, lay eggs on milkweed leaves, then die. The eggs hatch into caterpillars which soon develop into young butterflies, which continue their parents' flight north.

Watery feast

In the winter, *moose* browse on trees and bushes in forests across the far north of North America, Canada and Alaska. In summer, their main diet is water plants - they often wade up to their shoulders in marshy lakes to feed. Moose stand up to 2.3 m tall at the shoulder and need around 20 kg of vegetation a day to keep them going. In the harsh winter, many die of starvation or get stranded in deep snow and fall prey to wolves.

Singing frog

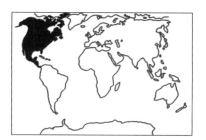

Living in damp woodland habitats in the eastern USA, the *spring peeper* is a tree frog only 2 cm long. Sticky pads on its long, thin fingers and toes give a good grip while it climbs trees in search of insect prey. In spring the male fills a sac in his throat with air, then 'peeps' or chirps to attract a mate. A chorus of thousands of peepers is an early sign of spring.

Ear ear

Owls have acute hearing and large, very light-sensitive eyes. They fly silently with down-covered flight feathers that muffle the air passing through them. With its wailing call, the *eastern screech owl* roosts in a hole in a tree and hunts at night for insects, birds and squirrels. Its ear tufts express its mood: raised when the owl is excited and flattened when at rest.

Knock on wood

A rapid drumming noise often signals the presence of a *pileated woodpecker*. This long-bodied bird with short legs has a distinctive red crest. It grips the bark of a tree with its strong claws, supports its body with its tail and drills into dead wood for insects such as the carpenter ant. The spongy bone at the base of the woodpecker's beak acts as a cushion against the hammering.

Landscape artist

The industry of the *beaver* controls floods, slows erosion and creates new wetlands. With their huge incisor teeth, beavers fell trees, which they nudge and float into position across fast-flowing streams. Then they build dams with sticks, stones and mud. The area behind the dam is flooded, creating a large pool. The beaver builds a nest called a lodge, with an underwater entrance, in the middle of the pool. Here, the beaver family can shelter from predators and cold weather.

Prickly customer

Long toe claws and an excellent sense of balance help the *North American porcupine* climb trees in search of new shoots and fruit. By night, it sleeps in a hollow tree. If attacked, it erects its spines and lashes its barbed tail from side to side. The loosely attached spines stick into the predator's flesh and slowly work their way in deeper. However, enemies such as bobcats and wolverines are skilled at flipping porcupines over and attacking their soft underbelly.

NORTH AMERICA

Two huge mountain ranges – the Rockies and Appalachians – run north to south on opposite sides of North America. In the west, the Rocky Mountains stretch for 5,150 km, from Alaska to Mexico. They include over 700 mountains of over 3,050 m – the highest peak, at 6,194 m, is in Alaska. The higher you go, the colder and wetter it becomes. At the lowest levels, mixed forests are home to white-tailed deer, porcupines and red foxes. In the higher coniferous forests, black bears forage for roots and berries, while predatory cougars and wolves roam. Above the tree line, summer alpine meadows are rich in insects which provide food for mountain bluebirds. Sure-footed mountain goats and bighorn sheep descend from rocky crags to graze with pikas and marmots. The Rockies and its national parks provide a refuge for animals that have been lost from other parts of North America.

In the east, the Appalachians stretch for about 2,400 km, from Quebec in Canada to Alabama in the USA. The Appalachians do not reach above 2,050 m, but their northern areas experience some of the worst winter weather on Earth. The Appalachians have the same life zones as the Rockies, although the warmer, southern peaks do not rise above the tree line. Here, animals such as white-tailed deer and spotted skunks are found on both upper and lower slopes.

Winter sleep

The *American black bear* eats plants, insects and fruits, but it will also take grubs, rodents, carrion and fish. Its sharp claws are used for digging, tearing food and climbing trees. It goes into a winter sleep in a tree hollow lined with dry plants. Born blind and naked in January, the cubs are suckled until they are ready to leave the den and learn to forage for themselves.

Headbanging

In the rutting season, male *bighorn sheep* charge and butt heads, reeling back dizzily after the collision. Sometimes they tussle with their long, curling horns in a desperate battle for territory and a mate. The horns of the female are much shorter. Bighorns are agile climbers and can leap nimbly from crag to crag. Their cloven (divided) hooves separate into two halves to help them grip the rocks.

White signal flag

The *white-tailed deer* is widespread in mountains and forests. It uses its short, white tail as an alarm signal for other deer. At the approach of danger, it flicks its tail up and down, and the small herd instantly darts away. The white tails may also help the deer follow each other. In summer, white-tailed deer eat grasses, fruits, nuts and blossoms. In winter, they use strong cheek teeth to browse on twigs.

Scaling the peaks

Herds of *North American mountain goats* live in the snowfields and near the glaciers of the Rockies. In the snow, they are camouflaged from predators like wolves and cougars by their warm, white coats. Their curved toes help them cling to steep, slippery slopes. When the kids are born, they scramble to their feet and in a few days are ready to leap across the rocks with the herd.

Grass harvest

Pikas live singly or in pairs among the rocks in remote mountainous areas. They make a nest in a crack or crevice. In summer and autumn, they eat grasses, shoots and flowers while collecting stores of food for the winter. They call out to defend their territory from intruders, but dart for cover among the rocks if threatened.

Food chain

The *northern goshawk* hunts in upland meadows and at the forest edge. It either manoeuvres in low flight through the trees or waits on a perch and swoops down on its victim. It preys mainly on other birds in flight, but also eats small mammals, such as pikas. Pikas, in turn, live off juicy plant material, including grass, leaves and new shoots.

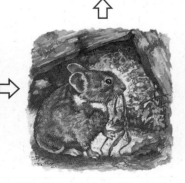

Scent marks

The *bobcat* marks its territory with scrapes, urine and droppings. By sniffing a female's urine, a male knows when she is ready to mate. Her droppings tell other females if she has kittens. Mother bobcats are very aggressive when defending their young. Bobcats hunt at night for rabbits and hares, creeping up silently until close enough to pounce, then killing them with a bite to the base of the neck.

PRAIRIE

NORTH AMERICA

The word prairie comes from the French for 'large meadow', but the North American prairies are more than large. They range from the Great Lakes in the east to the Rockies in the west, and from the dry Mexican plateau to the Canadian forests, covering 1.47 million square km. They are bitterly cold in winter and baking hot in summer. They were once just grasslands as there was not enough rain for trees to grow. As Europeans settled in North America in the 19th century, the prairies were turned over for agriculture.

The prairie soil, among the richest in the world, was used to grow wheat, corn and other cereals. Other areas were grazed by cattle and sheep, pushing out the native prairie species. The large grassland mammals, the bison and the antelope-like pronghorn, were almost wiped out by farming. Today, intensive agriculture has left few areas of natural prairie, although efforts are being made to restore it by planting native grasses. In natural prairie, ground-dwellers are the most common animals in the tree-less landscape. Ground squirrels, such as prairie dogs, live in extensive burrows, where they hibernate through the winter. While feeding on grasses, they may be taken by birds of prey such as the red-tailed hawk, by burrowing owls or by a coyote. This dog relative eats a wide variety of prey that also includes ground-living birds such as the sage grouse and the prairie chicken.

Offensive weapon

The *striped skunk* is a night hunter that feeds on insects and small mammals. It is generally solitary and spends the day in a burrow or sheltered spot. When threatened, the skunk turns its back on its enemy, raising its bushy tail, scratching with its front feet and hissing loudly. If the enemy does not retreat, the skunk then sprays a stinking, stinging fluid at its opponent's eyes from the anal gland in its bottom.

Long-distance runner

Distinguished by its mournful howl, the *coyote* is a relative of the wolf. It lives alone and hunts at dusk, scavenging on carrion or eating jackrabbits, prairie dogs and other rodents. It will sometimes hunt deer as a pack. Strong legs and a keen sense of smell help the pack follow prey for long distances and outrun it at speeds of 65 km/h. As the victim tires, the coyote moves in for the kill with its sharp-toothed jaws.

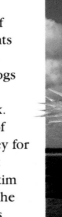

Puffed up

The male *sage grouse* displays to rival males to win a territory and also a mate. He puffs out his breast, inflates air sacs in his neck and makes popping calls. The winner attracts the female that is looking on. When they hatch, the young follow their mother, who teaches them to eat seeds and insects. It gets its name from the sagebrush plant on which it also feeds.

Peep hole

The *burrowing owl* makes its home underground. It can dig with its feet and beak, but prefers to move into an abandoned prairie dog hole. It hunts mainly at night, swooping down on its prey from the air or from a perch. It eats rodents, insects, lizards, snakes and birds. By day, it can be seen outside its burrow, but shelters inside if disturbed. It can turn its head through 180 degrees for all-round vision.

Squirrel city

The *prairie dog* is in fact a burrowing squirrel. One male, a harem of females and their young all live in a burrow as a family group, called a cotery. A network of tunnels connects the coteries into a huge underground city, home to thousands of animals. Their numbers are declining as their habitat is taken over for farms and other human uses.

Suit of armour

The horny plates of the *common long-nosed armadillo* protect it from predators. If attacked, it lies flat with its legs tucked in, or rolls into a ball. A night-hunter, the armadillo trots around snuffling for roots or small animals, which it digs out with its long, curved claws. It also licks insects out of their nest holes with its sticky tongue.

Saved from extinction

Great herds of *bison* once cropped their way across the prairies. But by 1880, nearly 60 million of these magnificent creatures had been shot by hunters and only 500 remained. Almost extinct, the bison were given protected grazing in national parklands, and today there are 25,000. Bison roam in herds of up to 50 animals and can live to be 40 years old.

WESTERN DESERTS

NORTH AMERICA

North America's desert regions extend from northern Mexico into the southwestern United States. The western deserts are parched, rocky and barren. When it rains, the water rapidly evaporates or disappears into the ground. The deserts are also hot for much of the year. Death Valley, which is one of the hottest places on Earth, with temperatures of up to 54°C, is part of the western deserts. It links the Great Basin Desert to the more southerly Mojave Desert. South of the Mojave is the Sonoran Desert, famous for its giant saguaro cacti.

Most desert animals shelter during the day in burrows or under stones, cacti or other plants, and come out at night to feed when it is cooler. Fruits, flowers, seeds – and the water-storing stems of cacti – provide both food and water for the insects and small mammals that can survive in the harsh desert environment. Plant-eating insects provide food for scorpions, spiders and the trap-building antlion larva, as well as lizards and the elf owl. Small mammals that forage for seeds, such as rodents, are prey for the rattlesnake and a poisonous lizard called the gila monster. Larger plant-eaters, such as jackrabbits and mule deer, are always alert to the approach of bobcats and other predators as they feed on tough grasses and cacti.

Bony shell

The shell of the *desert tortoise* is made of bony plates fused together. The upper part is called the carapace, and the lower part is the plastron. The shell protects the animal from the desert Sun. If threatened, the tortoise draws its head and legs back into its shell until the danger has passed. As it has no teeth, it tears at plants with the sharp edges of its jaws. It reproduces by laying eggs in the sand.

Black-tailed jackrabbit

○ This is a hare, which lives above ground, sheltering in a shallow scrape called a form.
○ Enormous ears give it acute hearing and act as a radiator to give off heat.
○ Males fight in spring for a mate.
○ To avoid predators, females hide young in different places.
○ Jackrabbits rarely drink water. They get moisture by nibbling succulent cacti.

Antlion

○ So called because of its fierce larvae, which have huge mouthparts for grabbing prey.
○ Digs a pit in the sand and waits at the bottom for prey to tumble in.
○ Eats worms, caterpillars, ants, spiders and centipedes.
○ Seizes prey with big, saw-like jaws, injects enzymes (proteins) and sucks out the juices.
○ Adult has long, delicate lacy wings and feeds on insects.

Gila monster

○ One of only two lizards with a poisonous bite.
○ Black and yellow colouring warns animals to stay away.
○ Produces poison in its lower jaw, which enters its victim as it bites and chews.
○ Eats lizards, snakes, eggs and small mammals and birds.
○ Heavy body and thick tail. Stores fat in its tail, and lives off this when food is short.

Roadrunner

○ Gets its name because it runs along roads and open ground in search of prey.
○ It can fly, but prefers to run. Reaching speeds of 30 km/h, it can run faster than most of its predators.
○ Tail is used as a brake and for steering.
○ When it catches a snake or lizard, it pecks it to death then swallows it head-first.
○ Also eats insects and fruit.

Hairy monster

Male *tarantulas* emerge from their shelter at dusk and wander the desert looking for food or a female. They mate in a burrow, where the female then lays her eggs. It can take ten years for a tarantula to grow into an adult. Like other spiders, it moults (sheds it skin) as it grows. It uses the poison in its bite to catch insects, then sucks the juices out from inside its prey. The hairs on the tarantula's body are irritating to predators and help deter them.

Detective snake

The *western diamondback rattlesnake* finds its prey in different ways. Its eyes let in lots of light for good vision. It flicks out its forked tongue to taste the air for its prey. It has pit organs – heat-sensitive membranes between its eyes and nostrils. These detect slight changes in temperature that tell the snake the position of a warm-blooded animal.

FLORIDA EVERGLADES

The subtropical Everglades is the world's largest wetland. It is largely grass-covered marshland, dotted with ponds and islands of trees. The Everglades (mostly contained within a national park) covers about 6,000 square km of the southern tip of the Florida peninsula. It provides a rich feeding and breeding area for many animals. The shallow fish-filled ponds, which are called 'gator holes because they are widened and deepened by American alligators, attract fish-eating water birds such as herons and spoonbills.

The richness of animal life in the Everglades depends on the flooding that takes place after the dry winter months. In the north, heavy rains cause Lake Okeechobee to overflow, and this forms a river 15 cm deep and 80 km wide which covers the Everglades. As the runoff spreads, water levels rise and river animals move freely throughout the park. An explosion of wildlife, including insects and small fish, provides food for larger animals.

Among the many species living in the park are 150 species of fish, 60 species of amphibians and reptiles – including American alligators and crocodiles – and over 300 bird species, including the snail-eating Everglade kite and fish-eating osprey. The few mammal species include the endangered Florida panther and water-living manatee. As the marshes dry out in winter, the animals gather around the 'gator holes that are vital to the way the environment works. Unfortunately, the pressures caused by the expanding human population in southern Florida pose a serious threat to this wilderness.

Glorious mud

The *American alligator* digs out the swamp to keep it flooded and well stocked with prey (freshwater turtles, fish and snakes). Alligators mate in the water and the female lays her eggs in a mound of rotting vegetation. The eggs stay warm inside the mound and when the young hatch, the mother opens it up. The babies are independent from birth and are mature when they are 2 m long, at about six years old.

Sea cow

In the summer, *manatees* feed on the seagrass meadows of the Gulf of Mexico. In autumn, they migrate to the lagoons and estuaries of the Everglades and eat freshwater plants. Manatees are often called sea cows because of the way they graze underwater. They digest their food slowly and belch a lot. Manatees have poor eyesight, but they call to each other to keep in touch.

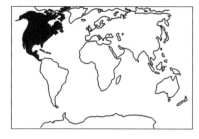

Pink legs

Like flamingoes, the *roseate spoonbill* has pink legs and feathers because of its diet of shrimp and other shellfish. Flocks of spoonbills can be seen wading through the mangroves searching for food. They sweep their bill from side to side in the water, snapping up food by touch. They settle in colonies to breed, and build untidy nests in the tree tops.

Snail lover

The *Everglade kite* is also called the snail kite because it feeds almost exclusively on just one type of water snail, the apple snail. It flies low over the water, watching out for snails clinging to the water plants, or spots its prey from a perch. Then it swoops and snatches the snail from the water with one of its feet. The Everglade kite holds the snail in its long, curling claws and uses its slender, hooked beak to winkle the creature from its shell. It nests in colonies and searches for food in groups.

In the swim

The *anhinga* swims underwater with only its sharp bill and curved neck above water. It could be mistaken for a swimming snake, which is why it is also called the snakebird. The anhinga catches fish by spearing them on its bill, then brings them to the surface to swallow whole. After eating, it comes ashore to spread its wings and dry them in the Sun.

Heat sensors

One of many water snakes that live in the Everglades, the *cottonmouth* is aggressive and dangerously venomous. It belongs to the family of pit vipers. When hunting at night, it uses heat sensors situated in pits in its head to locate its prey. Also called the water moccasin, the cottonmouth eats fish, frogs, salamanders, other snakes, birds and small mammals. It kills them with poisonous fangs.

Under threat

For nine months of the year, floodwaters from Lake Okeechobee in the north fill the swamps and marshlands of the Everglades. But in the 1980s, a huge drainage programme was begun, to take water from the lake for use in cities and to irrigate farmland. Now this unique environment and the many species that live there are under threat. Created a World Heritage Site in 1979, the Everglades is dependent on conservation efforts for its survival.

SOUTH AMERICA

South America is the world's fourth largest continent, with an area of about 17.8 million square km. Sitting between the Pacific and Atlantic Oceans, it extends over 7,000 km, from tropical Panama – its link to North America – southwards to the icy wastes of Cape Horn. Until two million years ago, South America was separate from North America and developed a unique set of animals, such as sloths, opossums, New World monkeys and anteaters. South America also has the world's richest bird life. Around one-third of all bird species breed here and, including winter visitors, nearly half the world's bird species spend some time here. Over 700 species are unique to South America, including rheas, hoatzins and antbirds.

The richest diversity of animals lives in the vast tract of tropical forest that covers the basin of the mighty Amazon River. These lush, dense forests in the north of the continent are home to millions of species, many of them insects and other invertebrates. Most of these have not yet been discovered or named. The Andes mountains – the backbone of the continent – run down the west side, from Venezuela to Chile. Between the central section of the Andes and the Pacific is the hot Atacama desert, one of the driest places on Earth – in some parts it has not rained for hundreds of years. Grasslands, including the pampas, fill much of the central and southern parts of South America.

Andes

The *spectacled bear* is the only South American bear, and is named for the rings round its eyes. Each one has different 'spectacles'. Active at night, they live in the grasslands and humid forests on the lower slopes of the Andes. Excellent climbers, they use their large paws and strong claws to climb trees, tear off branches, climb back down and eat the leaves and fruit. They sleep by day in a tree in a rough nest of sticks, or shelter in a den under a tangle of roots.

Amazon

The brightly coloured *poison dart frogs* are tropical forest-dwellers. Predators are warned off by their bold markings. Females lay eggs on wet leaves. When they hatch, the frogs carry the babies to pools inside cup-shaped bromeliads (which grow on trees), where they develop further. As the frogs grow, their colours develop and their skin starts to produce one of the deadliest-known animal poisons. Native Americans can tip 40 arrows with the poison from one frog, and this is how they get their name. Each arrow will paralyse an animal without making it dangerous to eat.

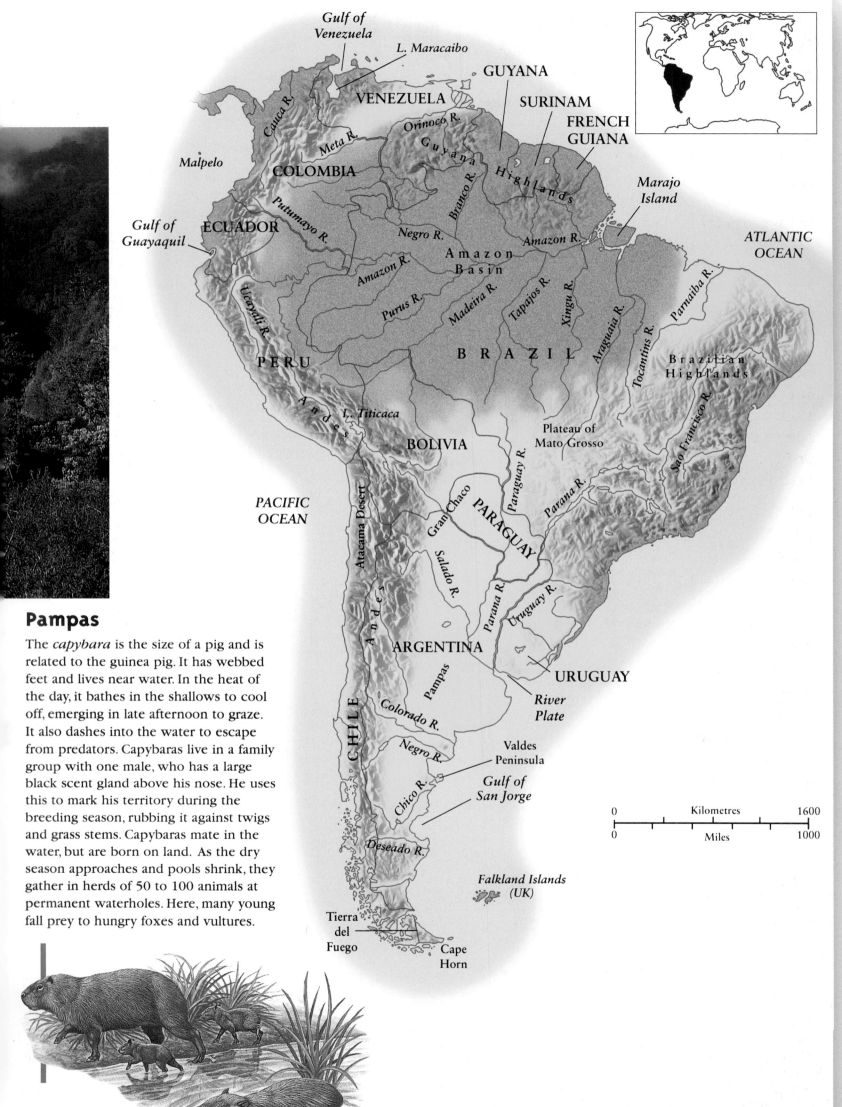

Gulf of
Venezuela

L. Maracaibo

GUYANA

VENEZUELA

SURINAM

FRENCH
GUIANA

Cauca R.

Orinoco R.

Guyana

Highlands

Marajo
Island

Meta R.

Malpelo

COLOMBIA

Branco R.

ATLANTIC
OCEAN

Gulf of
Guayaquil

ECUADOR

Putumayo R.

Negro R.

Amazon R.

Amazon
Basin

Amazon R.

Parnaiba R.

Purus R.

Madeira R.

Tapajos R.

Xingu R.

Araguaia R.

Tocantins R.

B R A Z I L

Brazilian
Highlands

PERU

Ucayali R.

Andes

L. Titicaca

Sao Francisco R.

BOLIVIA

Plateau of
Mato Grosso

PACIFIC
OCEAN

Atacama Desert

Gran Chaco

PARAGUAY

Paraguay R.

Parana R.

Salado R.

Andes

Parana R.

Uruguay R.

ARGENTINA

Pampas

URUGUAY

River
Plate

Colorado R.

CHILE

Negro R.

Valdes
Peninsula

Chico R.

Gulf of
San Jorge

Deseado R.

Falkland Islands
(UK)

Tierra
del
Fuego

Cape
Horn

| 0 | Kilometres | 1600 |
| 0 | Miles | 1000 |

Pampas

The *capybara* is the size of a pig and is
related to the guinea pig. It has webbed
feet and lives near water. In the heat of
the day, it bathes in the shallows to cool
off, emerging in late afternoon to graze.
It also dashes into the water to escape
from predators. Capybaras live in a family
group with one male, who has a large
black scent gland above his nose. He uses
this to mark his territory during the
breeding season, rubbing it against twigs
and grass stems. Capybaras mate in the
water, but are born on land. As the dry
season approaches and pools shrink, they
gather in herds of 50 to 100 animals at
permanent waterholes. Here, many young
fall prey to hungry foxes and vultures.

SOUTH AMERICA

The world's longest mountain chain, the Andes, runs for over 7,250 km down the western side of South America. The Andes have two parallel cordilleras (chains); the higher western peaks plunge steeply into the Pacific Ocean, while the eastern cordillera slopes more gently towards the Atlantic. The western slopes are dry, while the eastern have more rain, vegetation and animals. Many peaks are snow-covered and always shrouded in mist; the highest – Aconcagua in Argentina – reaches 6,960 m. Deforestation, cultivation and overgrazing cause severe soil erosion, but national parks, such as the Manu in Peru, are going some way to reversing this.

The eastern slopes witness a dramatic change in climate, vegetation and wildlife with increasing altitude. The lower slopes are covered in tropical forest, home to the spectacled bear, northern pudu and the shy Andean tapir. Within a few thousand metres, the hot, humid forest gives way to rocky slopes – home to the mountain viscacha – and then to snow-covered peaks. The two cordilleras are separated by a high plateau, or altiplano, covered by grassland or scrubland and dotted with lakes. The grasslands provide grazing for the vicuña, and for its domesticated relatives, the llama and alpaca. These and other high-altitude mammals are adapted for cold nights and for life in air that is low in oxygen. The lakes and wetlands of the altiplano are rich in fish and water birds.

High flyer

Like all vultures, the *Andean condor* has a bald head and neck so it can feed deep in the carcasses of dead animals without getting its feathers bloody. The world's largest bird of prey, it has a wingspan of 3.2 m. The condor soars on hot air currents high over the Andean foothills, looking for carrion. Its diet also includes fish. Because of poor food supply and poisoning by ranchers, the condor is getting scarce. The female lays only one egg at a time and it takes two years to rear a chick.

Andean flicker

○ A type of woodpecker that probes under bark for insects.
○ Catches ants on its long, sticky tongue.
○ Its feet are well adapted for climbing trees – two toes pointing forwards and two backwards to grip the bark.
○ Uses its beak to bore a nest hole in the puya plant. The puya has vicious spines, but makes a popular perch.

Northern pudu

○ Smallest of the world's deer, only 38 cm high at its shoulder.
○ Lives in the lower Andean forests and in the swampy savanna that stretches across the mountain foothills.
○ Simple antlers, long coarse hair and slender hooves.
○ Secretive animal that feeds on leaves, shoots and fruit.
○ Females give birth to single calves or twins.

Mountain viscacha

○ Looks like a long-tailed rabbit, and in some areas is called a 'rock squirrel'.
○ Found in dry, rocky terrain with sparse vegetation.
○ Families live in clefts and crevices in the rocks, forming colonies of up to 75 individuals.
○ Eats most plants including grasses, mosses and lichens.
○ Very agile across the rocks.

Giant hummingbird

○ At 23 cm long, the largest of the world's hummingbirds.
○ Builds a tiny nest of mosses and lichens on top of a branch or on a cactus stem.
○ Hovering flight allows it to sip nectar from flowers while it is on the wing; also perches on branches to feed.
○ Can use its long beak to probe for insects in bark or among debris.

Saved

The smallest member of the camel family, the *vicuña* grazes the high meadows of the Andes. Vicuñas were killed in large numbers for their valuable wool and hide and, by 1965, only 6,000 remained in the wild. Recent conservation programmes have saved the vicuña from extinction, and there are now about 85,000, mostly in national parks.

Athlete

The *cougar* has many names, including puma, mountain lion and panther. It lives all along the Andes, and is also found in North America. It prowls alone through mountain forests and scrubland in search of prey such as brocket deer. A fearsome hunter, the cougar has remarkable jumping power – it can leap 6 m into a tree and cover more than 10 m in one bound on the ground.

THE AMAZON RAINFOREST

The Amazon rainforest of Brazil, Colombia and northern Peru is the world's largest rainforest, covering nearly 6 million square km. It contains the greatest variety of animal life in the world, nearly half of all bird species – including 300 types of hummingbird – and an unknown number of insect species. The loud screeching of macaws fills the air, as do the booming calls of howler monkeys. Bright colours are everywhere, from the wings of butterflies to the warning patterns of poisonous frogs. The rainforest is hot, humid and wet all year round, ideal for the many different species of trees, creepers, ferns and epiphytes (plants that grow on trees), such as bromeliads.

The rich plantlife provides homes and food for the vast animal population. Each forest level has its own animal communities. Most live high in the canopy where the tree tops are exposed to the Sun. Here, flowers, fruit, leaves and insects provide food for monkeys, fruit bats, hummingbirds, opossums and toucans, all on the look-out for the fearsome harpy eagle. Lower down, snakes eat frogs and iguanas. Rainwater pools inside bromeliads provide drinking water and tadpole nurseries. On the forest floor, seed-eating rodents scuttle between the trees avoiding predators. The Amazon river and its tributaries are rich in life: many fish eat fallen fruit, while piranhas eat fish and animals that come to the water to drink.

Rare beauty

Ruthless hunting for their beautifully marked skin has wiped out *jaguars* in many areas. The jaguar hunts by stealth and ambush, mainly at night, eating anything from mice to tapirs. An excellent swimmer, it catches fish by flipping them out of the water with its paw. The jaguar lives alone, and males and females meet only to mate. Cubs stay near the den until around six months old, when they accompany their mother on hunting trips. After three years, they can hunt for themselves and are independent. Jaguars, like all rainforest animals, are threatened by the loss of their habitat through fire, logging and clearance for farming.

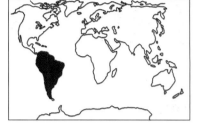

Nutcracker

The largest of South American parrots, the *scarlet macaw* feeds on fruit and nuts, using its foot as a 'hand' to hold its food. Its hooked beak is strong enough to crack the toughest nut of all, the Brazil – a food source unavailable to other birds. Macaws pair for life and bond by preening and 'kissing'.

Stripper

Piranhas hunt by smell, and the scent of blood will drive them into a frenzy. They will attack a shoal of fish or any animal. Small fish are eaten whole. Piranhas use their needle-sharp teeth and strong jaws to tear chunks off larger prey – they can cut through bone in a single bite and strip all the flesh off an animal the size of a pig in a minute.

Upside down

The *three-toed sloth* sleeps by day, eats leaves by night, mates and gives birth, all hanging upside down in a tree by its long, hooked claws. It can turn its head through 270 degrees so that it can see all round without moving. The sloth is slow-moving and may live in the same tree for years, descending to the forest floor weekly to defecate. In the hot, humid forest, green algae grow on its fur, which helps to keep it camouflaged from predators.

Blue jewel

The brilliant upper wings of the *blue morpho butterfly* flash as it takes off, startling any predators. Also, its patterned hind wings help to break up its

outline, so it is less of a target for hungry birds. The underside of its wings, displayed when it is at rest with its wings folded up, are dull brown. This camouflages the morpho, making it blend into the tree bark. The blue morpho is hunted by collectors for use in jewellery.

Monkey-eater

The dominant bird of prey in the South American rainforest is the largest and most powerful eagle in the world, the *harpy eagle*. Up to a metre from head to tail, the harpy eagle can reach speeds of up to 80 km/h as it chases prey. It can carry off creatures as large as monkeys and sloths in its huge, powerful talons, and also feeds on opossums and snakes.

Action needed

The destruction of the Amazon rainforest – for hardwood timber, mining and farmland – could wipe out half the world's animal species, many native peoples and a vast wealth of plants that may supply the cures for countless diseases. Burning the forest is also increasing levels of carbon dioxide gas in the atmosphere. At the current rate of destruction, no forest will be left at all by 2035.

THE PAMPAS

East of the Andes, there are 1.3 million square km of temperate grassland, the best known area of which is the pampas of Argentina and Uruguay. The pampas once occupied over 430,000 square km. In the wetter eastern pampas, a lot of land has been taken over for cereal farming. In the drier west, 300 years of cattle grazing has removed many of the native grasses, sedges and shrubs. The pampas wildlife is not as rich as in the tropical forests, but it is home to many species that are found here and nowhere else. Many of these species are adapted to the open terrain. The few large plant-grazers – apart from domesticated cattle – include the rare pampas deer.

Further north, the water-loving capybara grazes on grasslands near water. Smaller grazers include the mara and viscacha, both related to the guinea pig. Like many smaller animals that have no trees or bushes to shelter in, they go underground. Other burrowers include insect-eating armadillos. Giant armadillos, which lash out with their sharp front claws if attacked, feed on termites. These insects live in massive colonies inside towering nests dotted around the pampas landscape. There are many ground-dwelling birds, like the rhea and the crested caracara. As well as cougars, larger predators include the maned wolf, whose long legs enable it to see over tall grasses when hunting for prey.

Blood feast

The fierce-looking *vampire bat* is not much bigger than a sparrow. It feeds mainly on the blood of cattle, pigs and horses. Active by night, it bites its victim then laps blood from the wound. Its saliva stops the blood from clotting. The vampire bat is considered a pest by farmers, as it can pass on diseases like rabies to their livestock.

Tight squeeze

The *boa constrictor* cannot catch fast-moving prey. It hunts by lying in wait or sliding silently up to its victim. It wraps its tail round the animal's body, constricting (squeezing) it, until it can no longer breathe. The boa's 'elastic' jaws can open wide enough for it to eat a wild pig or a capybara whole. After a big meal, it will not need to eat for a week.

Air-conditioned

Termites are soft-bodied insects that feed on plant material. They live in colonies in a termitarium (huge tower), which they build using a mixture of soil and saliva. This sets like cement. At the heart of the colony lives a bloated, egg-laying queen. Workers build foodstores, air shafts, fungus gardens and passages to the outside world. These are guarded by sentries, which let workers in and out.

Ruffled feathers

The tousled plumage of the *rhea* is one sign that this bird cannot fly – only flying birds need a streamlined shape. Another clue is the long, muscular legs, well-adapted to racing across grasslands to outpace predators. The male mates with several females, then builds a nest in which they lay their eggs. He incubates the eggs and rears the young, caring for them for up to five months. Rheas eat seeds, insects and small animals.

Sprinter

The *mara* is also called the Patagonian hare, but it is in fact a rodent. It can leap 2 m and runs at 45 km/h to escape its predators. It feeds by day on grass, shoots, leaves and fruit. The mara digs its own burrow or takes one over from another animal, like the viscacha. Mara numbers are declining, particularly where a competitor, such as the introduced European hare, is found.

Home-breaker

The *giant anteater* feeds on ants and termites. Its tongue, which is covered in spines and saliva to trap insects, extends about 60 cm – over half its body length. A giant anteater needs to eat 30,000 insects a day and may visit 40 nests. It tears open a termite mound with its huge claws but does not destroy it, so it can return to feed again. The anteater protects its claws by walking on its knuckles.

Competition

The animals of the pampas now compete with grazing herds of livestock, particularly beef cattle, for their food. Intensive farming with too many cattle in small areas of pasture has led to overgrazing and damage to the pampas ecology. Farmers protecting their herds and pastures with guns are an added threat. As ranching has increased, many native animal species have disappeared, including the jaguar. Other species, including the giant anteater, are frequently shot on sight, even though they are not pests or of any commercial value.

AUSTRALASIA

Australasia includes Australia, New Zealand and the surrounding islands, as well as Papua New Guinea (the eastern half of the island of New Guinea). Lying between the Indian and Pacific Oceans, Australia is the world's smallest continent, with an area of just 7.7 million

Tropical North

The *spotted cuscus* is a tree-living marsupial from the rainforests of New Guinea and the Australian north. It feeds at night on leaves, flowers and fruit, and also eats small reptiles and birds. An excellent climber, the cuscus clings to the branches with its feet and its prehensile (gripping) tail. During the day, it rests high up in the trees hiding from predators.

square km. Australia has been isolated for some 30 million years, and has many unique animals, including the world's greatest variety of marsupial, or pouched, mammals such as kangaroos and koalas. Marsupials, found also in New Guinea and the Americas, give birth to tiny, underdeveloped young that complete their development in their mother's pouch. Australia also has as a wide range of birds, reptiles, insects and spiders.

Australia is mostly hot, dry desert, grassland and scrub, known collectively as the outback. Marsupial mice, emus and wallabies are adapted to these hot, dry conditions. To the east of the Great Dividing Range, the climate is milder, with hot summers and cooler winters. New Guinea and northeastern Australia have tropical forests.

A rich variety of animals live here, like the cuscus and tree kangaroo. New Zealand has a warm, wet climate with few native mammals. Introduced species like rabbits, cats and foxes have affected and wiped out some of Australasia's native wildlife.

Outback

The *brown falcon* hunts by watching motionless from a high perch, then swooping down on its prey. With its long legs and broad wings, it is one of the biggest falcons, but it tackles small prey. It feeds on small mammals, reptiles, insects and young or injured birds, gripping them with its powerful talons and ripping their flesh with its beak. It has a harsh, cackling call and the females are larger than the males.

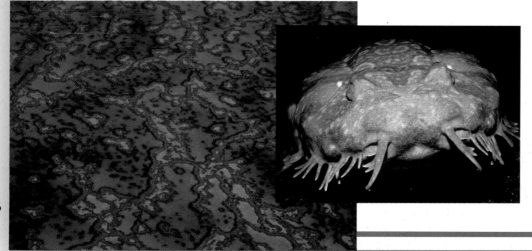

Great Barrier Reef

The *wobbegong* or carpet shark lurks on the sea bed, waiting to feed. It is camouflaged by its mottled brown, grey and yellow colouring and by the protrusions (growths) around its mouth. When a small fish swims nearby, the wobbegong makes a sudden lunge forward and sucks its prey into its mouth. It has two to five rows of small, razor-sharp teeth. These do not pierce the prey deeply, but clamp down hard on it so that it cannot escape.

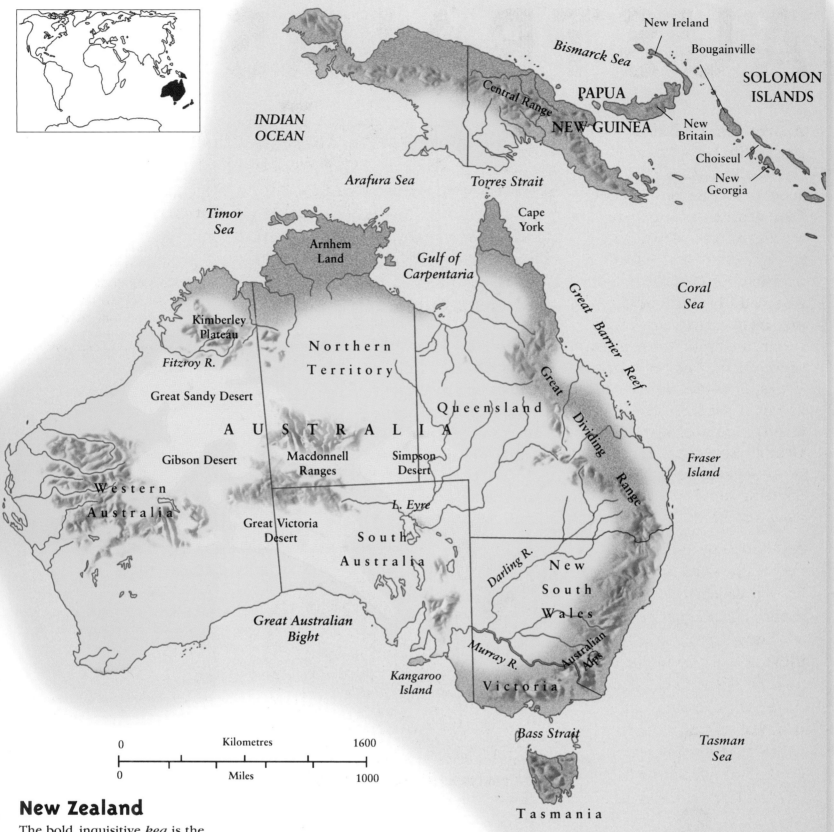

INDIAN OCEAN

Bismarck Sea

New Ireland

Bougainville

SOLOMON ISLANDS

PAPUA NEW GUINEA

Central Range

New Britain

Choiseul

New Georgia

Arafura Sea

Torres Strait

Timor Sea

Cape York

Gulf of Carpentaria

Coral Sea

Arnhem Land

Kimberley Plateau

Fitzroy R.

Great Sandy Desert

N o r t h e r n   T e r r i t o r y

Great Barrier Reef

Q u e e n s l a n d

Great Dividing Range

A U S T R A L I A

Gibson Desert

Macdonnell Ranges

Simpson Desert

Fraser Island

W e s t e r n   A u s t r a l i a

Great Victoria Desert

L. Eyre

S o u t h   A u s t r a l i a

Darling R.

N e w   S o u t h   W a l e s

Great Australian Bight

Kangaroo Island

Murray R.

V i c t o r i a

Australian Alps

Bass Strait

Tasman Sea

T a s m a n i a

0		Kilometres		1600
0		Miles		1000

New Zealand

The bold, inquisitive *kea* is the only meat-eating parrot. It is named after its call, 'kee-ah'. It is heavily built and can be seen near houses and farms, where it feeds on small mammals and dead animals, using its long, hooked beak to rip the flesh. It is a powerful flier, but spends a lot of time on the ground, scratching for grubs and insects. It also eats seeds, leaves, nectar and fruit. It makes its nest in a rocky crevice and lines it with grass, twigs and chewed wood. The young form flocks, but adult males live in a territory with up to four females.

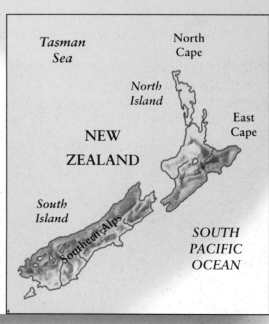

Tasman Sea

North Cape

North Island

East Cape

NEW ZEALAND

South Island

Southern Alps

SOUTH PACIFIC OCEAN

67

THE TROPICAL NORTH

AUSTRALASIA

The northeastern part of Australia and mountainous New Guinea – the island some 2,200 km long that lies off its coast – share the same hot and wet climate and the same rainforest vegetation. The many species of ferns and trees found in the forest provide homes and food for a huge array of unusual animals. Australia's rainforests cover only 0.1 per cent of the continent, yet contain 30 per cent of its frogs, two of the three species of monotreme (egg-laying mammal), 30 per cent of its marsupials, 62 per cent of its butterflies and a large proportion of its bats, birds and reptiles, including the deadly poisonous taipan snake.

Much of the forest is now protected as a World Heritage Site, which is intended to prevent wholesale destruction in the future. However, the introduction of alien species, such as the cane toad, has affected native animals, such as the carnivorous quoll, which is poisoned by the toad's skin secretions.

The rainforests of New Guinea and Australia have a rich variety of canopy-living animals, including brightly coloured lorikeets and cuscuses which feed on fruit, flowers and leaves, as well as sugar gliders – marsupials that glide from tree to tree.

Bright camouflage

The bright green male *eclectus parrot* and the red and blue female were once thought to be different species. Their brilliant plumage provides excellent camouflage in the colourful canopy of New Guinea's rainforest. The male is difficult to spot in the tree tops, searching for nuts, fruits and seeds. The female disappears into the shadows as she incubates her eggs in a nest hole in a tree.

Hard hat

A flightless *cassowary* uses its small wings to help it balance while running and for breeding time displays. Instead of feathers, the wings are covered in bare quills. It has a bony crest called a casque; this protects its head when it runs through the undergrowth to escape predators. The female may pair with more than one male, laying a clutch of eggs for each. The boldly striped chicks are cared for by their father for nine months.

Climbing marsupial

The *tree kangaroo* is well adapted to life in rainforest trees. It has shorter hind legs and longer forelegs than its ground-dwelling relative. Its sharp, curved claws and the rough pads under its feet are used for gripping tree bark. Its long tail helps it to balance and steer as it scrambles and leaps through the trees in search of juicy leaves and fruit. It is active at night; by day, it curls up to sleep on a branch.

Flower power

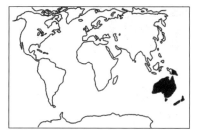

Southern blossom bats use their tongue to feed on flower nectar and pollen, which showers down on them and sticks to their fur. Visiting another flower of the same species, they rub against it and pollination occurs. Unlike insect-eating bats that rely on echolocation to find prey, blossom bats and other fruit bats use their nose and eyes to lead them to food.

Deadly venom

One of the world's most poisonous snakes, the *taipan* injects deadly venom deep into its prey with its 1 cm fangs. Taipans are shy and solitary and rarely seen. In winter, they lie coiled up in sheltered dens. The female taipan lays her eggs in a hollow in soft soil, and leaves them to hatch. Within days of hatching, the young snake kills its first prey.

Jewel of the forest

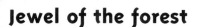

The *Raggiana* is the most spectacular of New Guinea's 40 birds of paradise. The males compete high in a rainforest tree. They flap their wings frantically, toss their spectacular display feathers and hang upside down in a shimmering frenzy. The female chooses the showiest bird to be her mate. Normally, just one or two dominant males do all the matings; the other males in the lek (display area) display in vain.

Bad mistake

The *cane toad* was introduced into Australia from South America in 1935 to eat cane beetles destroying the sugar cane plantations, but the experiment backfired. The toads failed to wipe out the beetles and became pests themselves, by eating native species including snakes, frogs, small mammals and birds. Cane toad numbers have increased rapidly because they have no natural enemies. Also, any animal that touches or attempts to eat the toad is poisoned by the toxic secretions released from glands behind its head.

THE OUTBACK

Most of Australia's people live on the coast, especially in the east and southeast. Of the rest of the country, nearly half is hot desert, and over a third is scrub or dry grassland – hot in summer and cool in winter – which surrounds the central desert. Together, these vast areas form the outback, a dry plateau that stretches from the west coast to the eastern mountains. In the outback, water is in short supply. Despite the harsh conditions, a wide range of animals thrives here, although only a fraction of the number found in Australia's eastern forests. Many survive on little or no water, and seek shelter during the day from the Sun.

Desert
Scrub

In the outback, drought-resistant plants like porcupine grass and acacia trees provide shelter and food for animals. There are many reptiles, such as goannas, skinks, frilled lizards and the bizarre-looking thorny devil, whose spiny skin gathers water droplets from the morning dew. Birds, such as cockatoos and parakeets, fly in flocks between scattered trees. The mammals range from meat-eating marsupial 'mice', such as dunnarts and mulgaras, to kangaroos and wallabies. Where grasslands are used for grazing by farmers, the vast herds of cattle and sheep compete for food with the native grazers. Introduced species, such as foxes and feral cats, have caused the extinction of some native marsupial species.

Gone wild

A member of the dog family and once a pet of the Aborigines, the *dingo* has been wild for many years. It is now regarded as a pest, as it sometimes preys on livestock. Family groups have a core territory, but may hunt over a wide area in a pack. After the dingoes have eaten their fill, they bury the leftover carcass for later.

Marsupial mouse

Dunnarts are sometimes called marsupial mice because of their size and pointed face. But, unlike mice, the *fat-tailed dunnart* eats insects and spiders caught during night-time hunts. In the wet season, it builds up food reserves in its tail. In the dry season, when food is scarce, the tail shrinks as the dunnart uses up its reserves. In a long drought, it rests under logs or rocks to make its food stores last longer.

Bouncy

Red kangaroos travel in mobs (groups) of up to 100, move at up to 56 km/h and can hop more than 12 m in a single bound. They graze, mainly on grass, resting on their shorter front feet. They usually feed and travel at night, with mothers carrying their young, called joeys, in their pouch. By day, they rest sheltering from the Sun.

Spiny egg-layer

The short-beaked *echidna* has no teeth or jaw muscles. It feeds by licking up ants and other insects with its sticky tongue. The echidnas and the duck-billed platypus are the only mammals that lay eggs. The female lays a single egg in a pouch on her abdomen. The baby hatches out of the leathery shell and feeds on her milk for about two months.

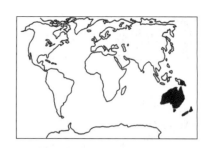

Big ruff

The *frilled lizard* uses surprise tactics to scare away enemies. It opens a coloured parasol of skin around its neck. This makes it look much bigger than it is. At the same time, it bobs its head with its mouth open to show the bright colour inside, hisses and lashes about with its tail. This can scare away predators such as the grey goshawk.

Blue neck

The flightless *emu* is Australia's biggest bird and can be 1.7 m tall. Its tiny wings are hidden under its long feathers and it strides about on long, muscular legs. The male has a low, booming mating call. The female lays her eggs in a hollow in the ground, and the male cares for the chicks. In some areas, the emu has become a pest. It eats almost anything and can trample sheep fences.

Protected

The *koala* was once hunted for its fur and faced extinction. Now it is protected and lives in the forests of eastern Australia. Koalas eat only eucalyptus leaves. There are more than 100 species of eucalyptus in Australia, but koalas will feed on only 12 of them. A koala eats up to 1 kg of not-very-nutritious leaves per night; during the day it rests for 18 hours to save energy. The koala's worst enemy is forest fire.

71

THE GREAT BARRIER REEF

The Great Barrier Reef is the largest coral reef in the world and can be seen from space. It extends for 2,000 km, from Papua New Guinea to the Tropic of Capricorn, off Australia's northeastern coast. Reefs grow in shallow tropical seas. A reef consists of the protective, chalky skeletons of tiny coral organisms related to sea anemones, called polyps. It takes hundreds of years for a reef to form. Polyps have two sources of food: they use their stinging tentacles to catch prey that floats past in the reef's currents, and they contain tiny plant-like algae, which make food from sunlight. Coral reefs are rich in animal life because they provide plentiful food, shelter and a place to breed.

The Great Barrier Reef contains over 400 species of coral, including brain corals, stag corals and delicate fan corals. Around 1,500 species of fish live here. The moray eel lies in wait for prey in coral crevices – other fish swim in large shoals, feeding on plankton and algae. Sharks patrol the reef, waiting for a fish to move away from its shelter. The reef also has over 4,000 species of mollusc, including sea slugs and octopuses that lurk in crevices before grabbing prey with their tentacles. Sea urchins, turtles and sea cucumbers are also common. The reef's status as a World Heritage Site should protect it from the damage done by tourists and divers who threaten reefs around the world.

Supershell

One of the world's largest invertebrates, at 400 kg and over 1 m long, is the *giant clam*. It lives in the shallows of the tropical Pacific Ocean. Its shell opens to feed, and shuts quickly when danger approaches. The opened shell is fringed by brightly coloured soft tissue. Its vivid greens and blues are produced by algae that form a relationship with the clam. The clam 'farms' the algae and gets nutrients from them, as well as filtering food particles from the water. The algae have a home in which to grow, reproduce and photosynthesise using the Sun's rays.

Long meal

The flattened tail of the *olive sea snake* acts like a powerful paddle to thrust it through the water after its prey. The female is larger than the male and feeds mainly on the bigger eels that live in deep water off the reef. The smaller males hunt for moray eels in the reef face. Their venom stuns their prey, which they then eat whole.

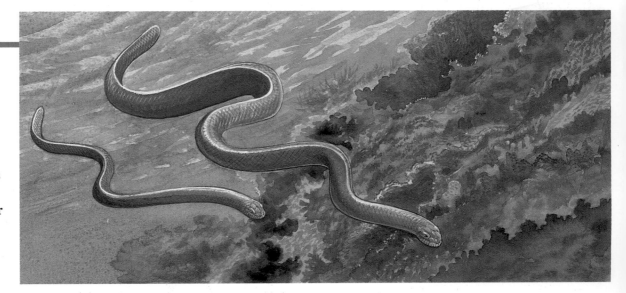

Clownfish

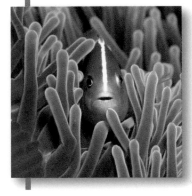

○ Has a special relationship with sea anemones and is immune to the sting in the anemone's tentacles.
○ When pursued by an enemy, it hides among the anemone's tentacles, which sting and devour its predator: the clownfish eats the leftovers.
○ Chases away butterfly fish, which prey on the anemone, by biting off the ends of its tentacles.
○ Cleans debris off the anemone and eats dead tentacles.

Brain coral

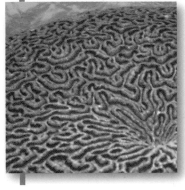

○ So called because it looks like a human brain – one of many types that make up the Great Barrier Reef.
○ Corals are the hollow skeletons of thousands of tiny animals, called polyps, which live together in colonies. These skeletons build up to form a reef.
○ A polyp looks like a sea anemone, with a ring of stinging tentacles that wave in the water to catch food.

Blue-streaked cleaner wrasse

○ So called because it removes parasites from other fish.
○ Bright colouring and swimming pattern attract the larger fish that it cleans.
○ Fish wait in line for the cleaner's services.
○ Large predators like the moray eel allow the cleaner wrasse to remove debris from between their teeth without harming it.
○ Also rids larger fish of dead or diseased tissue.

Tiger shark

○ Cruises off the reef, feeding on any marine prey. Sometimes presents a threat to divers exploring the reef.
○ Also feeds on sea snakes.
○ Jaws are loosely attached to its skull, so it can open them wide to take huge bites out of its prey with its razor-sharp teeth.
○ Worn-out teeth are continuously replaced by rows of newer ones.
○ May use as many as 30,000 teeth in a lifetime.

Endangered

The coral reef is a fragile habitat and its complex food web is easily disturbed. Reefs are threatened by overfishing. If the fish that graze on algae growing on the reef are removed, the corals become overgrown. Reefs worldwide are also damaged by souvenir hunters, boats and pollution, and smothered by silt that runs off the land. Much damage has been caused to the Great Barrier Reef by the *crown of thorns starfish* (below right), which eats the coral polyps. One starfish can destroy 1.8 square m of coral in a day. Coral reefs grow slowly and take hundreds of years to recover from damage.

Softie

Tubular sponges live on parts of the reef where there is plenty of food for them. They draw in water and filter out the nutrients. Branching varieties of sponge are found in still waters; more rounded forms grow where tides are stronger. Many small creatures thrive in and around sponges, such as tiny brittle-stars, crustaceans and worms, which feed on the food particles the sponge draws into itself.

NEW ZEALAND & TASMANIA

New Zealand is 1,600 km to the east of Australia, half way between the South Pole and the equator. There are two main islands – North and South – with smaller islands around them. The overall climate is mild, but part of North Island is subtropical, while parts of South Island have heavy snow in winter, and glaciers and fjords mark the landscape. Rich farmland is found on both islands. New Zealand became isolated about 80 million years ago, well before Australia, and before mammals became widely distributed. Therefore it has only two native species of mammal – both are bats. Without predators, many birds such as kiwis, takahes, keas and kakapos became flightless. Unfortunately, European settlers brought predators with them in the shape of rats, cats and dogs, and many native ground-dwelling birds are now found only in isolated areas or on small islands.

Map legend:
- Mixed forest
- Mountain
- Rainforest
- Scrubland

NEW ZEALAND

Big egg

The flightless *kiwi* forages by night in dense undergrowth. Unusually for a bird, it uses smell to find food, sniffing out grubs, insects and spiders with the nostrils at the end of its beak. It lays the biggest egg relative to its size of any bird. The male sits on the egg in his burrow for up to 12 weeks. After the incubation, the baby kiwi hatches and is ready to forage for food with its parents within a week.

Tasmania, the wettest and most mountainous part of Australia, lies 240 km off its southeastern coast. Like New Zealand and Australia, its native animals have suffered from the arrival of settlers and their animals. But it still has a wide range of marsupials, such as quolls and wombats, as well as the egg-laying platypus. The Tasmanian devil is also found here. Mystery surrounds the existence of the thylacine, the largest meat-eating marsupial. Once hunted near to extinction, it may have been wiped out by disease earlier last century, or – perhaps – a few may survive in isolated areas. The search goes on.

Living fossil

The *tuatara* is the sole survivor of a reptile group that lived alongside the dinosaurs. Today, it is found on only a few small islands. The female lays 5 to 15 eggs that hatch in 15 months. The young grow slowly and can live for 120 years. Tuatara means 'peaks on the back'– males raise these spines when alarmed. They shelter in burrows by day and hunt at night for worms, insects and spiders.

Surfers

At dusk in the breeding season, *fairy penguins* ride ashore on the surf, then waddle up the beach to join their chicks and mates in their burrows. The adults take turns to stay in the nest and go to sea to feed on fish and squid. They breed on the shores of New Zealand, Australia and Tasmania. They are fast and agile underwater, sometimes working together to round up shoals of small fish.

TASMANIA

Egg-laying mammal

Living beside quiet waterways in Tasmania and Australia, the *duckbilled platypus* is an excellent swimmer that forages underwater for crayfish, freshwater shrimps and insect larvae. It probes for prey in the stream bed using its sensitive bill. The female platypus makes a nest in the riverbank at the end of a long burrow and lines it with grasses. She lays two eggs. The young are 2.5 cm long when they hatch. They suckle milk from their mother, and stay in the burrow until they are ready to fend for themselves.

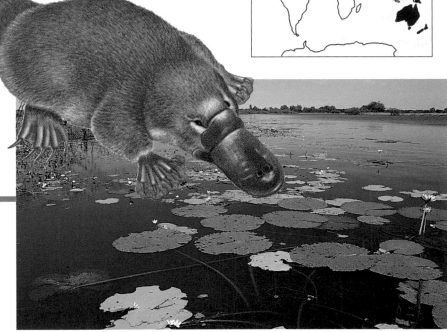

Little demon

The size of a small dog, the *Tasmanian devil* is so called because of its black coat and eerie wail and because it makes its prey disappear by eating every scrap. It has short, strong legs for foraging for reptiles and small mammals, and its powerful jaws and sharp teeth can crush bones. It also eats dead sheep and wallabies.

Hunting party

Now very rare, the *eastern quoll* is found in the dry forests of Tasmania. Emerging at night from a daytime home in a rock pile or hollow log, it hunts for small insects, birds, reptiles and rodents. The female quoll gives birth to up to 24 tiny young, but only the strongest survive. When they are older, they cling to her body and ride with her when she goes hunting.

Teeth that grow

Wombats live in burrows up to 20 m long and are active at night. The female carries her baby in a pouch that faces backwards. At six months, the wombat climbs out of its mother's pouch and forages with her for roots, grasses and fungi. Wombats have long, sharp teeth that grow continually as they get worn down by cropping the vegetation.

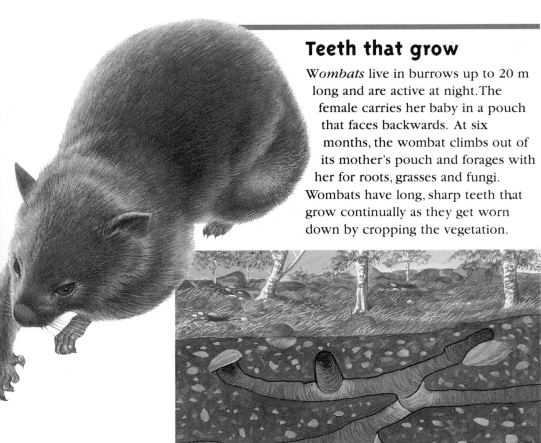

ANTARCTICA

The size of Europe and the United States combined, Antarctica is the windiest, coldest, driest and most isolated continent on Earth. During the long, dark winter, temperatures can drop to -89°C, and the wind can gust at 200 km/h. Antarctica is surrounded by seas and buried under a permanent icecap 4.8 km thick in places, which contains 90 per cent of the world's ice (70 per cent of its fresh water). The icecap extends over the ocean as sheets that retreat in summer and expand in winter. Only 2 per cent of Antarctica is ice-free and it is here that its only permanent residents – a few insects and mites – live.

However, the ocean around Antarctica teems with life, especially during the short summer. An upwelling of nutrients around the coast encourages the growth of phytoplankton (tiny plant plankton) that float near the surface. These provide food for zooplankton – especially shrimp-like krill – which feed crab, fish and squid. These are eaten by seals and penguins and they, in turn, are eaten by killer whales and leopard seals. Krill is also an important food for baleen whales like the blue whale. Many seals and seabirds take up temporary residence on land in summer to moult and breed. Current agreements protect Earth's last unspoilt wilderness by forbidding mining or oil exploration. But commercial fishing for krill – a major food source – could easily upset the fragile ocean ecosystem.

Giant bird

With a 3 m wingspan, the *wandering albatross* is a powerful flier. It masters southern ocean storms, soaring hundreds of kilometres in search of squid. It stores food as an oily liquid in its stomach to be digested later or regurgitated for its chick. It nests in small colonies on Antarctic islands and pairs for life, normally rearing one chick every two years. It matures after ten years and can live for 30 years.

Footsie

Emperor penguins breed on the winter ice surrounding Antarctica. The female lays a single egg, which the male incubates balanced on his feet for about 60 days. His mate goes to sea to feed. The males huddle together to withstand the cold. The female returns and feeds the chick with regurgitated fish. The male can then feed. At around three months, the chicks gather next to the water while both adults fetch food.

Fast mover

Adélie penguins eat krill and fish. To leave the water, they swim to shore and leap up to 3 m to land on the ice on their feet or stomach. Using their feet and flippers, they toboggan over the ice. Adélie penguins nest onshore in summer, in crowded colonies, each bird returning to the same mate and nest every year and rearing two young.

Dainty eater

The largest creature ever to have lived on the planet, the *blue whale* feeds in the summer months on krill. Instead of teeth, its mouth has rows of baleen plates fringed with bristles. The whale gulps in water, then forces it back out so that the baleen bristles sieve out the tiny prey, which it then swallows. In autumn, the whales move to warmer waters and do not eat for up to eight months.

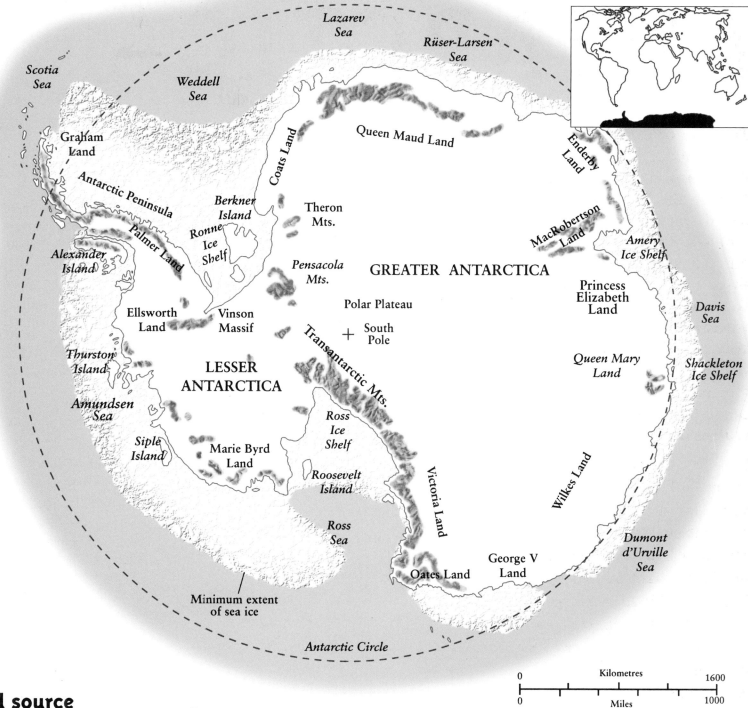

Lazarev Sea

Rüser-Larsen Sea

Scotia Sea

Weddell Sea

Graham Land

Queen Maud Land

Coats Land

Enderby Land

Antarctic Peninsula

Berkner Island

Theron Mts.

MacRobertson Land

Palmer Land

Ronne Ice Shelf

Amery Ice Shelf

Alexander Island

Pensacola Mts.

GREATER ANTARCTICA

Princess Elizabeth Land

Davis Sea

Ellsworth Land

Vinson Massif

Polar Plateau

+ South Pole

LESSER ANTARCTICA

Transantarctic Mts.

Queen Mary Land

Shackleton Ice Shelf

Thurston Island

Amundsen Sea

Ross Ice Shelf

Siple Island

Marie Byrd Land

Roosevelt Island

Victoria Land

Wilkes Land

Ross Sea

Dumont d'Urville Sea

Minimum extent of sea ice

Oates Land

George V Land

Antarctic Circle

| 0 | Kilometres | 1600 |
| 0 | Miles | 1000 |

Food source

Krill are finger-length, shrimp-like creatures. In summer, they are found close to the ocean's surface in swarms of many millions. Krill feed on plankton, filtering them out of the water with their feathery front legs. In turn, they provide food for many other creatures, such as the blue whale, which eats up to 4,000 kg of krill in a day. Krill breed quickly in these nutrient-rich waters. One female can lay 3,000 eggs a year.

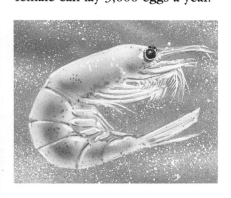

Foghorn

The largest seal in the world, a male *southern elephant seal* can weigh up to 4,000 kg. Elephant seals feed on fish and squid and can dive as deep as 1,500 m. In the breeding season, each high-ranking male guards a harem of up to 100 females. The male roars at rival males to stay away, amplifying the sound through the inflatable skin bag on his nose. If threats fail, the male will fight his rival.

Spotted hunter

The *leopard seal* patrols the edge of the pack ice. A ferocious hunter and a fast swimmer, it eats penguins, fish, krill, seals and their pups. Leopard seals spend most of their time in the freezing waters and have a thick layer of blubber which keeps them warm. They come to the surface to breathe and keep their nostrils open by scraping the ice off with their teeth.

GLOSSARY

Algae Simple plant-like living things, most of which live in water.

Amphibian Vertebrate that lives both on land and in water.

Arachnid Arthropod with four pairs of legs, such as a spider or scorpion.

Arthropod Invertebrate with jointed hard outer skeleton and limbs.

Backbone Flexible chain of bones that runs from head to tail of a vertebrate.

Baleen Fringed plates that hang from the roof of the mouth of the largest whales and filter their food.

Biodiversity Variety of living things in one area.

Biome Area such as savanna or tropical forest defined by its climate, plant life and associated animals.

Biosphere All regions on Earth – land, air and sea – inhabited by living things.

Camouflage Colours, patterns and shapes that make an animal hard to see against its background.

Canopy Top layer of branches and leaves that form the 'roof' of a forest.

Carnivore Meat-eater.

Carrion Dead animal eaten by scavengers.

Classification Method of identifying and grouping animals.

Climate Average weather conditions found in a particular region.

Colony Members of the same species that live together and interact.

Conifer Tree such as pine that reproduces by making seeds in cones.

Coral Tiny marine colonial polyps that produce a protective outer casing; over centuries these produce a coral reef.

Crustacean Arthropod such as lobster or crab with jointed legs and two pairs of antennae (feelers).

Deciduous Describes a tree that sheds its leaves in autumn.

Desert An area where very little rain falls, so few plants can grow.

Drought A long period without rain.

Echolocation System used by bats to determine the position of an object using timing and direction of echoes.

Ecology Study of relationship between living things and their environment.

Ecosystem The community of different animal and plant species found in a particular habitat.

Endothermic Describes animals – birds and mammals – whose bodies are kept at a constant warm temperature.

Food chain Food pathway linking different species in an ecosystem; energy flows along food chain from plants to plant-eaters to meat-eaters.

Food web Food chains linked together within an ecosystem.

Genus Group of one or more closely related species.

Gland An organ in an animal that produces chemicals. Some mammals have scent glands that give off a strong smell, used for marking territory.

Habitat Place where a species lives.

Herbivore Plant-eater.

Hibernation Sleep-like state used by some mammals to survive the cold winter months.

Incubate To sit on eggs and keep them warm until they hatch.

Invertebrate Animal without a backbone.

Larva The young of certain animals. Caterpillars are the larvae (plural) of butterflies.

Mammal Endothermic animal that has a covering of fur and feeds its young on milk. Most mammals give birth to well-developed young.

Marsupial Mammals that give birth to tiny, undeveloped young that grow inside a pouch.

Mating The coming together of a male and a female animal for reproduction.

Metamorphosis Change from one state into another as an animal develops into an adult, e.g. from a tadpole into a frog.

Migrate To travel from one area to another to find more favourable conditions, e.g. food.

Mollusc Soft-bodied invertebrate like a snail, often with a hard protective shell.

Monotreme Egg-laying mammal.

Pampas Grasslands of South America.

Photosynthesis The process by which plants make food using sunlight.

Placental Describes mammals that give birth to well-developed young.

Pollination Transfer of pollen from the male part of a flower to the female part; necessary for sexual reproduction and seed production.

Polyp Small tube-shaped animal with tentacles round its mouth; single polyps include sea anemones, colonial forms include the Portuguese man-of-war.

Prairie North American grasslands.

Predator Animal that hunts other animals for food.

Reproduction The production of offspring (young).

Reptile Vertebrate with waterproof scaly skin, such as a lizard, that typically lays eggs and lives on land.

Rodent A mammal with sharp incisors (front teeth) for gnawing, such as a mouse or squirrel.

Savanna Hot grasslands in Africa.

Scavenger Animal that feeds on the carcasses of other animals.

Species Group of similar living things that breed together in the wild.

Steppe Grasslands of Central Europe and Asia.

Taiga Northern coniferous forest of Europe and Asia.

Temperate A climate that does not have extremely hot summers or extremely cold winters.

Tentacle The 'arm' of an animal, such as an octopus, used for grasping.

Territory Area defended by an animal where it feeds and breeds.

Tropics The region of the Earth round the equator, which has a warm, wet climate all year round.

Tundra Land around the North Pole where the ground is frozen all year.

Tusk Tooth that sticks out of the jaw.

Venom Poison injected by one animal into another through fangs or a sting.

Vertebrate Animal with a backbone.

INDEX

Addax (Addax nasomaculatus) 36, 43
Adélie penguin (Pygoscelis adeliae) 76
Africa 4, 36–45
African elephant (Loxodonta africana) 39
African hunting dog (Lycaon pictus) 7, 38, 39
African jacana (Actophilornis africanus) 44
Alpine chough (Pyrrhochorax graculus) 19
Alpine marmot (Marmota marmota) 19
Amazon River 58, 59
American alligator (Alligator mississippiensis) 56
American black bear (Ursus americanus) 50
amphibians
  Asian horned frog 32
  Cane toad 69
  Edible frog 7, 23
  Fire salamander 25
  Poison-dart frog 58
  Spring peeper 49
Andean condor (Vultur gryphus) 60
Andean flicker (Colaptes rupicola) 61
Anhinga (Anhinga anhinga) 57
Antarctica 13, 14, 76–77
antelopes
  Addax 36, 43
  Impala 7, 36, 39
  Lechwe 44
  Wildebeest 5, 39
Antlion (Myrmeleon sp.) 55
apes
  Chimpanzee 7, 41
  Gibbon 32, 33
  Gorilla 37
  Orang-utan 34
Apollo butterfly (Parnassius sp.) 31
arachnids
  Scorpion 8, 38, 54
  Tarantula 55
Arctic 13, 14–15, 26
Arctic fox (Alopex agopus) 14
Arctic tern (Sterna paradisaea) 14
Asia 4, 14, 26–35
Asian horned frog (Megophrys montana) 32
Australasia 66–75
Australia 4, 16
Aye-aye (Daubentonia madagascariensis) 11

Baikal seal (Phoca sibirica) 29
bats
  Greater false vampire 35
  Southern blossom 7, 69
  Vampire 64
bears
  American black 50
  Brown 7, 17
  Polar 14
  Spectacled 58, 60
Beaver (Castor canadensis) 7, 49
Bighorn sheep (Ovis canadensis) 50

birds of prey
  Andean condor 60
  Brown falcon 66
  Burrowing owl 53
  Eastern screech owl 49
  Eurasian sparrowhawk 21
  Everglade kite 57
  Golden eagle 18, 19
  Great bustard 29
  Harpy eagle 7, 63
  Northern goshawk 51
  Secretary bird 39
  Verreaux's eagle 45
Bison (Bison bison) 53
Black rhinoceros (Diceros bicornis) 38
Black-tailed jackrabbit (Lepus californicus) 55
Blue morpho butterfly (Morpho retenor) 7, 62, 63
Blue-streaked cleaner wrasse (Labrodes dimidiatus) 73
Blue whale (Balaenoptera musculus) 76
Boa constrictor (Boa constrictor) 64
Bobcat (Lynx rufus) 7, 49, 51, 54
Brain coral (Symphylla radians) 73
Brown bear (Ursus arctos) 7, 17
Brown falcon (Falco berigora) 66
Burrowing owl (Speotyto cunicularia) 53
butterflies
  Apollo 31
  Blue morpho 7, 62, 63
  Common blue 21
  Monarch 48

Camargue horse (Equus caballus) 25
camels
  Dromedary 43
  Vicuña 61
Cane toad (Bufo marinus) 69
Capybara (Hydroch0erus hydrochaeris) 59
Cassowary (Casuarius casuarius) 68
cats
  Bobcat 7, 49, 51, 54
  Cheetah 7, 44
  Cougar 7, 50, 61
  European wild cat 7, 16
  Jaguar 62
  Leopard 6, 7, 38, 40
  Lion 5, 6, 7, 38, 39, 44
  Snow leopard 31
  Spanish lynx 7, 24
  Tiger 6, 7, 26, 33
Chamois (Rupicapra rupicapra), 19
Cheetah 7, 44
Chimpanzee (Pan troglodytes) 7, 41
Cichlid 45
Clownfish (Amphiprion percula) 7, 73
Colugo (Cynocephalus variegatus) 27
Common blue butterfly (Polyommatus icarus), 21
Common long-nosed armadillo (Dasypus novemcinctus) 53

Cottonmouth (Agkistrodon piscivorus) 57
Cougar (Puma concolor) 7, 50, 61
Coyote (Canis latrans) 52
Crossbill (Loxia curvirostra) 18
Crown of thorns starfish (Acantaster planci) 7, 73
crustaceans
  Fiddler crab 7, 13
  Krill 76, 77
Dabb spiny-tailed lizard (Uromastyx acanthinurus) 43
deer
  Moose 48
  Musk 26
  Northern pudu 60, 61
  Red 21
  White-tailed 50, 51
deserts
  Kalahari 37, 42
  Mojave 54
  Namib 37, 42
  Sahara 4, 37, 42
  Sonoran 54
Desert horned viper (Cerastes cerastes) 42
Desert jerboa (Jaculus orientalis) 4, 42
Desert tortoise (Gopherus agassizi) 54
Dingo (Canis dingo) 70
dogs
  African hunting 7, 38, 39
  Arctic fox 14
  Coyote 52
  Fennec fox 43
  Grey wolf 28
  Kit fox 47
Dragonfly (Aeshna cyanaea) 23
Dromedary (Camelus dromedarius) 43
Duck-billed platypus (Ornithorhynchus anatinus) 75
Dung beetle (Scarabaeus sacer) 6, 43

Eastern quoll (Dasyurus viverrinus) 75
Eastern screech owl (Otus asio) 49
Echidna (Tachyglossus aculeatus) 71
Eclectus parrot (Eclectus roratus) 68
Edible frog (Rana esculenta) 7, 23
Emperor penguin (Aptenodytes forsteri) 76
Emu (Dromaius novaehollandiae) 71
Eurasian badger (Meles meles) 21
Eurasian jay (Garrulus glandarius) 16
Eurasian otter (Lutra lutra) 16
Eurasian sparrowhawk (Accipiter nisus) 21
Europe 4, 14, 16–25, 76
European hedgehog (Erinaceus europaeus) 20
European mole (Talpa europaea) 21
European wild cat (Felis

silvestris) 7, 16
Everglade kite (Rostrhamus sociabilis) 57

Fairy penguin (Eudyptula minor) 74
farmland 20–21, 46, 52, 57, 63, 64, 65, 70, 74
Fat-tailed dunnart (Sminthopsis crassicaudata) 70
Fennec fox (Fennecus zerda) 42
Fiddler crab (Uca pugilator) 7, 13
Fire salamander (Salamandra salamandra) 25
fish
  Blue-streaked cleaner 73
  Cichlid 45
  Clownfish 7, 73
  Marlin 13
  Nile perch 44, 45
  Pike 22
  Piranha 63
flightless birds
  Adélie penguin 76
  Cassowary 68
  Emperor penguin 76
  Emu 71
  Fairy penguin 74
  Flightless cormorant 10
  Kiwi 74
  Ostrich 39
  Rhea 58, 64, 65
Flightless cormorant (Nannopterum harrisi) 10
forests 4, 5, 16, 18, 26, 32–33, 44, 46, 48–49, 50, 52, 70
Frilled lizard (Chlamydosaurus kingi) 71

Gaboon viper (Bitis gabonica) 41
Galápagos giant tortoise (Geochelone elephantopus) 10
Gecko (Hemidactylus turcicus) 24
Gelada (Theropithecus gelada) 45
Giant anteater (Myrmecophaga tridactyla) 65
Giant clam (Tridacna sp.) 72
Giant hummingbird (Patagona gigas) 61
Giant panda (Ailuropoda melanoleuca) 30
Gibbon (Hylobates lar) 33
Gila monster (Heloderma suspectum) 55
goats
  Chamois 19
  Markhor 31
  North American mountain 51
Golden eagle (Aquila chrysaetos) 19
Golden pheasant (Chrysolophus pictus) 30
Gorilla (Gorilla gorilla) 37
grasslands
  pampas 58, 59, 64–65
  prairie 5, 46, 52–53
  savanna 5, 36, 44
  steppe 5, 26, 28–29

Great bustard (Otis tarda) 29
Greater false vampire bat (Megaderma sp.) 35
Greater flamingo (Phoenicopterus ruber) 25
Great white shark (Carcharodon carcharias) 12
Grey parrot (Psittacus erithacus) 40
Grey wolf (Canis lupus) 28

Hanuman langur (Semnopithecus entellus) 27
Harpy eagle (Harpia harpyja) 7, 63
Hermann's tortoise (Testudo hermanii) 25
Heron (Ardea cinerea) 23
Hill mynah (Gracula religiosa) 31
Hippopotamus (Hippopotamus amphibius) 44
Honeyguide (Indicator indicator) 41
horses
  Camargue 25
  Onager 29
  Zebra 4, 5 38

icecaps 76–77
Impala (Aepyceros melampus), 7, 36
insects
  Apollo butterfly 31
  Blue morpho butterfly 7, 62, 63
  Common blue butterfly 21
  Dragonfly 22, 23
  Dung beetle 43
  Monarch butterfly 48
  Pine processionary moth 25
  Praying mantis 41
  Stag beetle 55
  Termite 40, 42, 65
  Wood ant 18

Jaguar (Panthera onca) 62

Kea (Nestor notablis) 67
King cobra (Ophiophagus hannah) 33
Kingfisher (Alcedo atthis) 22
Kit fox (Vulpes macrotis) 47
Kiwi (Apteryx australis) 74
Koala (Phascolarctos cinereus) 71
Komodo dragon (Varans komodoensis) 7, 35
Krill (Euphausia superba) 77

lakes
  Baikal 27, 29
  Great Lakes 46, 47, 48, 52
  Okeechobee 57
  Victoria 37, 45
Lechwe (Kobus lechwe) 44
lemurs
  Aye-aye 11
  Ring-tailed 11
Leopard (Panthera pardus) 6, 7, 38, 40
Leopard seal (Hydrurga leptonyx) 77
Linnaeus, Carolus 6, 7
Lion (Panthera leo) 5, 6, 7, 38, 39, 44

lizards
  Dabb spiny-tailed 43
  Frilled 70, 71
  Gecko 24
  Gila monster 54, 55
  Komodo dragon 7, 34, 35
  Marine iguana 10
  Parson's chameleon 11
  Tuatara 74

Malay tapir (Tapirus indicus) 32
Manatee (Trichechus manatus) 56
Mara (Dolichotis patagona) 65
Marbled polecat (Vormela peregusna) 26
Marine iguana (Amblyrhynchus cristatus) 10
Markhor (Capra falconeri) 31
Marlin (Makaira nigricans) 13
marsupials
  Koala 71
  Red kangaroo 7, 70
  Tasmanian devil 75
  Tree kangaroo 66, 69
  Virginia opposum 46, 48
  Wombat 75
Mediterranean monk seal (Monachus monachus) 24
Mediterranean sea 16, 17, 24
Meerkat (Suricata suricatta) 7, 36
molluscs
  Giant clam 72
  Octopus 7, 13, 72
Monarch butterfly (Danaus plexippus) 48
Mongolian gerbil (Meriones unguiculatus) 29
monotremes
  Duck-billed platypus 71, 75
  Echidna 71
Moose (Alces alces) 48
mountains
  Alps 16, 17, 18
  Andes 58, 59, 60-61, 64
  Caucasus 17, 26, 27
  Great Dividing Range 66, 67
  Himalayas 26, 27
  Pyrenees 16, 17, 18
  Rift Valley 40
  Rockies 46, 50-51
  Urals 16, 17, 26, 27
Mountain bluebird (Sialia currocoides) 46
Mountain viscacha (Lagidium sp.) 61
Mudskipper (Periophthalmus

chrysospilus) 35
Musk deer (Moschus moschiferus) 26

Nile crocodile (Crocodylus niloticus) 37
Nile perch (Lates niloticus) 45
North America 4, 14, 26, 46-57
North American mountain goat (Oreamnos americanus) 51
North American porcupine (Erethizon dorsatum) 49
Northern goshawk (Accipter gentilis) 51
Northern pudu (Pudu mephistophiles) 61

oceans
  Arctic 13, 14, 15, 16, 27
  Atlantic 13, 17, 24, 46, 47, 58, 60
  Indian 13, 27, 66, 67
  Pacific 10, 13, 27, 46, 47, 58, 60, 66, 67
Octopus (Octopus vulgaris) 7, 13, 72
Olive sea snake (Aipysurus laevis) 72
Onager (Equus hemionus) 29
Orang-utan (Pongo pygmaeus) 34
Ostrich (Struthio camelus) 39

Palm civet (Paradoxurus hermaphroditus) 32
Pangolin (Manis tricuspis) 40
parrots
  Eclectus 68
  Grey 40
  Kea 66, 74
  Scarlet macaw 45
Parson's chameleon (Chamaeleo parsonii) 11
Pika (Ochotona princeps) 51
Pike (Esox lucius) 22
Pileated woodpecker (Dryocopus pileatus) 49
Pine marten (Martes martes) 29
Pine processionary moth (Thaumetopoea pityocampa) 25
Piranha (Serrasalmus nattereri) 63
Poison-dart frog (Phyllobates terribilis) 58
Polar bear (Ursus maritimus) 14

Portuguese man-of-war (Physalia physalis) 7, 13
Prairie dog (Cynomys ludovicianus) 53
Praying mantis (Polyspilota sp.) 41
Purple gallinule (Porphyrio martinica) 47
Pyrenean desman (Galemys pyrenaicus) 19

Raggiana bird of paradise (Paradisaea raggiana) 69
rainforests 5, 6, 32-33, 40-41, 58, 62, 63, 68
Ratel (Mellivora capensis) 41
Red deer (Cervus elephas) 21
Red junglefowl (Gallus gallus) 33
Red kangaroo (Macropus rufus) 7, 70
reefs 5, 6 34, 72
Rhea (Rhea americana) 65
rhinoceros
  Black 38, 44
  Sumatran 34
Rhinoceros hornbill (Buceros rhinoceros) 35
Ring-tailed lemur (Lemur catta), 11
Roadrunner (Geococcyx californicus) 55
Rock hyrax (Procavia sp.) 45
rodents
  Alpine marmot 19
  Beaver 7, 49
  Black-tailed jackrabbit 52, 54, 55
  Capybara 59, 64
  Desert jerboa 4, 43
  Eurasian badger 21
  Eurasian otter 16, 22
  European hedgehog 20
  European mole 21
  Fat-tailed dunnart 70
  Mara 64, 65
  Meerkat 7, 36
  Mongolian gerbil 29
  Mountain viscacha 60, 61, 64
  North American porcupine 49, 50
  Pika 51
  Prairie dog 52, 53
  Pyrenean desman 19
  Raccoon 7, 48, 52
  Rock hyrax 45
  Siberian lemming 14, 15, 28
  Suslik 29
  Water shrew 22, 23
Roseate spoonbill (Ajaia ajaja) 57

Sage grouse (Centrocercus urophasianus) 53
Scarlet macaw (Ara macao) 63
Scarlet-tufted malachite sunbird (Nectarinia famosa) 45
Scorpion (Pandinus sp.) 38
Seahorse (Hippocampus sp.) 13
seals
  Baikal 29
  Southern elephant 77
  Walrus 15
Secretary bird (Sagittarius serpentarius) 39
sharks
  Great white 12
  Tiger 7, 73
  Wobbegong 75
Siberian lemming (Lemmus sibiricus) 15
Snow goose (Anser caerulescens) 14
Snow leopard (Uncia uncia) 31
South America 4, 58-65
Southern blossom bat (Syconycteris australis) 7, 69
Southern elephant seal (Mirounga leonina) 77
Spanish lynx (Lynx lynx) 24
Spectacled bear (Tremarctos ornatus) 58
Sponge (Clatharia sp.) 6, 7, 8
Spotted cuscus (Phalanger maculatus) 66
Spring peeper (Hyla crucifer) 49
Stag beetle (Lucanus cervus) 21
Stork (Ciconia ciconia) 25
Striped skunk (Mephitis mephitis) 52
Sumatran rhinoceros (Dicerorhinus sumatrensis) 34
Suslik (Spermophilus citellus) 29

taiga 5, 26, 28-29
Taipan (Oxyuranus scutellatus) 69
Tarantula (Aphnopelma chalcodes) 55
Tasmanian devil (Sarcophilus harrisii) 75
Termite (Cornitermes sp.) 65
Three-toed sloth (Bradypus tridactylus) 63
Tiger (Panthera tigris) 6, 7, 26, 33
Tiger shark (Galeocerdo

cuvieri) 7, 73
tortoise
  Desert 54
  Galápagos 10
  Hermann's 63
Tree kangaroo (Dendrolagus lumholtzi) 69
Tuatara (Sphenodo punctatus) 74
Tubular sponge (Aplysina archeri) 73
tundra 5

Vampire bat (Desmodus rotundus) 64
Verreaux's eagle (Aquila verreauxi) 45
Vicuña (Vicugna vicugna) 61
Virginia opossum (Didelphis virginiana) 46

Walrus (Odobenus rosmarus) 15
Wandering albatross (Diomeda exulans) 76
water birds
  African jacana 44
  Anhinga 57
  Greater flamingo 25
  Heron 22, 23
  Kingfisher 22
  Purple gallinule 47
  Roseate spoonbill 57
  Snow goose 14
  Stork 25
  Wandering albatross 76
Water shrew (Neomys fodiens) 23
Western diamondback rattlesnake (Crotalus atrox) 55
wetlands 16, 22-23, 44-45, 46
White-tailed deer (Odocoileus virginianus) 51
Wild boar (Sus scrofa) 18
Wildebeest (Connochaetus taurinus) 5, 39
Wobbegong (Orectolobus ornatus) 66
Wombat (Vombatus ursinus) 75
Wood ant (Formica rufa) 18
Woodpecker finch (Camarhynchus pallidus) 10

Yak (Bos grunniens) 31

Zebra (Equus burchelli) 38

Abbreviations: t-top, m-middle, b-bottom, r-right, l-left, c-centre

Artwork credits: Map artwork - Stephen Sweet. 4b, 5bl, 7mr, 7br, 7br, 8mt, 10bm, 19mt, 22ml, 23tl, 23mr, 23br, 24bl, 25tl, 25t, 25tm, 25tr, 25bm, 29br, 29tm, 33ml, 40m, 41br, 46bl, 47bl, 54mt, 61tr, 68m, 69tr, 69tl, 69br, 72b, 73tr, 73ml, 75br, 75bm, 76br, 77br - Terry Riley. 7ml, 7m, 29tr, 49m, 49mr, 49ml, 49br, 64bl, 65bl, 65mr, 65br, 76bl - Andrew Tewson. 7m, 7mr, 26br, 27br, 32bm, 32bl, 35ml, 40bl, 43ml, 61tm, 61tl, 70br - Dave Burroughs. 7ml, 7mr, 7mr, 8m, 8ml, 9bl, 9bm, 14br, 14bl, 18m, 18bl, 20m, 44bl, 44br, 45ml, 45bl, 45tr, 66tm, 66mr, 67bm - Stan Peach. 16tm, 16bm, 19m, 19bl, 57m, 57mr - Rob Shone. 7ml, 30br, 31ml, 31bl, 31mr, 36mt, 51mr, 51br, 53ml, 53bl, 53mr - Stephen Angel. 7tr - Dan Woods. Additional artwork by: Peter Barrett, James Field, Karen Johnson, Ian Moores, Jonathon Pointer, John Rignall, Chris Shields, Michael Taylor, Myke Taylor, George Thompson.

Photograph credits: 1, 7tll, 7tm, 7mlr, 11bl, 16t, 17bl, 25mr, 33t, 33mt, 62, 63mt - John Foxx Images. 2, 7rb, 8br, 36t, 38l, 38r, 39tl, 44 both, 45tr, 55l, 66c, 66bl, 67, 68mr, 68br, 69ml, 70l, 70bl, 71tl, 71mr - Corbis. 7cr, 29t - Michael Callan. 7bm, 7br, 7c, 7ctl, 7ct, 7ctr, 8l, 12 both, 13 both, 14tr, 14c, 15, 19br, 24mr, 26bl, 28, 31tr, 31br, 34l, 34r, 36mt, 36bl, 37b, 38bl, 38br, 39r, 39bl, 43tl, 46mr, 48br, 50bl, 51 all, 52b, 53tl, 53c, 53br, 54, 56, 60b, 61b, 69c, 70c, 71tr, 71br, 73bl, 73tm, 76c - Digital Stock. 7ml, 39mtl - Jurgen and Christine Sohns/FLPA - Images of Nature. 7cb, 16b, 17br, 18ml, 20br, 22bl, 22mr, 24br, 25ml, 26t, 29br, 31c, 34t, 48br, 49tl, 49mr, 73tl, 73mr - Stockbyte. 9c, 9mb, 35r, 55l, 57 both, 63mr - Royalty Free/CORBIS. 11c -Wolfgang Kaehler/CORBIS. 11br - Nick Garbutt/BBC Natural History Unit. 20bl - Roger Tidman/CORBIS. 21tr - RSPB Images. 21br, 61mr - Hubert Stadler/CORBIS. 21mr, 23tr - Brian Hunter Smart. 23br - Roger Tidman/FLPA - Images of Nature. 24l - Steve Kaufman/CORBIS. 26c - Yossi Eshbol/FLPA - Images of Nature. 27, 65t - Peter Oxford/BBC Natural History Unit. FLPA/CORBIS. 29ml - Doug Allen/BBC Natural History Unit. 32c - Michael & Patricia Fogden/CORBIS. 32mt, 34c - Anup Shah/BBC Natural History Unit. 35t, 42bl - Kevin Schafer/CORBIS. 39mtr, 41mr, 42ml, 42br - David Hosking/FLPA - Images of Nature. 41tl - Chris Hellier/BBC Natural History Unit. 43br - J. Tinning/FLPA - Images of Nature. 45mr - Charles Philip Cangialosi/CORBIS. 45tm - Keith Scholey/BBC Natural History Unit. 49bl, 55tl - Darrell Gulin/CORBIS. 51r - Thomas Lazar. 58mr, 74b - Mark Newman/FLPA - Images of Nature. 59tr - Michael Hollings/FLPA - Images of Nature. 61ml - Panda Photo/FLPA - Images of Nature. 61t - George Lepp/BBC Natural History Unit. 64t - Jim Clare/BBC Natural History Unit. 64br - Derk Hall/FLPA - Images of Nature. 65mr, 75c - Martin B. Withers/FLPA - Images of Nature. 66bm - Jeff Rotman/BBC Natural History Unit. 69mr - Dennis Degnan/CORBIS. 71ml - Foto Natura Stock/FLPA - Images of Nature. 72 - Jeffrey L. Rottman/CORBIS. 74c, 75tr - Tom and Pam Gardner/FLPA - Images of Nature. 30 both, 33b, 77 - Lynn M Stone/BBC Natural History Unit.